BRITISH BUS FLEET S

Rear-Engined Double-Deckers

Gavin Booth

LONDON
IAN ALLAN LTD

Contents

First published 1987

ISBN 0 7110 1687 9

Published by Ian Allan Ltd, Shepperton, Surrey; and printed by Ian Allan Printing Ltd at their works at Coombelands in Runnymede, England

Front cover:
Leyland Titan demonstrator in use with West Midlands PTE in May 1978. John Robinson

Back cover:
A Plymouth City Transport Leyland Atlantean AN68B/1R with East Lancs body.
John Robinson

Introduction

There has always been a great deal of interest in Britain in the types of bus on the market, and recently there has been a growing interest in how well these have sold and who buys them.

This first *British Bus Fleet Survey* covers rear-engined double-deckers, a type familiar throughout the country since the early 1960s. This book covers the period from 1970 in greater detail, although the background history is given to set the scene for those who were not around at that time.

The year 1970 is a convenient dividing-line. In the late 1960s the British bus industry had undergone major changes, with the bringing together of former rival groups Tilling and British Electric Traction (BET) under the new National Bus Company (NBC); the creation of Passenger Transport Executives (PTEs) in four major conurbations; the hiving-off of London Transport's outer area to form London Country; and the Government's Bus Grants scheme which encouraged operators to buy certain preferred types of bus. Each of these factors played its part in subsequent events. On a more practical level, the period since 1970 is just slightly longer than the life of an average full-size bus, so readers should be familiar with most of the buses and bus operators mentioned.

There have been so many changes in the structure and ownership of the bus-operating industry over the past 20 years, that readers may become confused by some of the present fleetnames of undertakings, and may be unable to relate them to some of the fleets represented in this book. As this is written, new names are being adopted for some of the newly-privatised former NBC subsidiaries, but since this book is particularly concerned with the period since 1970 it is not necessary to cover these.

It *is* important, though, to understand the structure of the municipal and PTE operators, since their influence has been strong in double-deck vehicle design.

At the start of 1969 there were 89 municipal bus fleets in Great Britain, but the 1968 Transport Act had created Passenger Transport Executives in four major English conurbations, and the process of forming these had started by the end of 1969. The first four PTEs, with their constituent municipalities and subsequent changes were:

West Midlands PTE (formed 1/10/69): Birmingham, Walsall, West Bromwich, Wolverhampton. Coventry added 1/4/74. Became West Midlands Travel plc, 1986.

SELNEC PTE (South-East Lancashire, North-East Cheshire) (formed 1/11/69): Ashton-under-Lyne, Bolton, Bury, Leigh, Manchester, Oldham, Ramsbottom, Rochdale, Salford, SHMD Board, Stockport. Wigan added 1/4/74. Became Greater Manchester PTE, 1974 and Greater Manchester Buses Ltd, 1986.

Merseyside PTE (formed 1/12/69): Birkenhead, Liverpool, Wallasey. St Helens and Southport added 1/4/74. Became Merseybus Ltd, 1986.

Tyneside PTE (formed 1/1/70): Newcastle, South Shields. Sunderland added 1/4/74. Became Tyne & Wear PTE, 1974, and Busways Travel Services Ltd, 1986.

Greater Glasgow PTE (formed 1/6/73): Glasgow. Became Strathclyde PTE, 1980, and Strathclyde Buses Ltd, 1986.

South Yorkshire PTE (formed 1/4/74): Doncaster, Rotherham, Sheffield. Became South Yorkshire Transport Ltd, 1986.

West Yorkshire PTE (formed 1/4/74): Bradford, Halifax/Calderdale, Huddersfield, Leeds. Became Yorkshire Rider Ltd, 1986.

The remaining municipal fleets, with older names in brackets for recognition, are: Barrow-in-Furness, Blackburn (Blackburn, Darwen), Blackpool, Bournemouth, Brighton, Burnley & Pendle (Burnley, Colne & Nelson), Cardiff, Chester, Chesterfield, Cleveland (Teesside, formerly Middlesbrough, Stockton, TRTB), Colchester, Cynon Valley (Aberdare), Darlington, Derby, Eastbourne, Fylde (Lytham St Annes), Grampian (Aberdeen), Great Yarmouth, Grimsby Cleethorpes, Halton (Widnes), Hartlepool, Hyndburn (Accrington), Ipswich, Islwyn (West Mon), Kingston-upon-Hull, Lancaster (Lancaster, Morecambe & Heysham), Leicester, Lincoln, Lothian (Edinburgh), Maidstone, Merthyr Tydfil, Newport, Northampton, Nottingham, Plymouth, Portsmouth, Preston, Reading, Rhymney Valley (Bedwas & Machen, Caerphilly, Gelligaer), Rossendale (Haslingden, Rawtenstall), Southampton, Southend, Taff-Ely (Pontypridd), Tayside (Dundee), Thamesdown (Swindon), Warrington.

Aberconwy (Llandudno) and Colwyn (Colwyn Bay) gave up bus operation in 1985. Other municipalities that have disappeared since 1969 have been Exeter (to NBC in 1970, and to Devon General), Luton (to United Counties 1970) and Waveney (Lowestoft) (to Eastern Counties 1976/77). In 1985 the East Staffordshire undertaking was merged with local independent Stevenson of Uttoxeter.

After the general background, the major rear-engined double-deck models are covered in detail, with a specification, chassis drawing (complete vehicle in the case of integrally-constructed buses), and notes on the model and the market.

Then there are chapters on double-deck coaches, double-deck bodywork, and evaluation tests carried out involving the models described in this book.

Several sources have proved useful in providing background material, notably the regular *Commercial Motor* bus fleet surveys, and the figures compiled from PSV Circle data by Paul Heels of the Polytechnic of Central London. Inevitably, there are discrepancies between these figures, and figures supplied by manufacturers or the Society of Motor Manufacturers and Traders (SMMT), but I have attempted to choose the most representative figures in each case.

I would like to thank the photographers who willingly supplied material for consideration, and Stewart Brown, who kindly read through the manuscript and made several useful additions and amendments.

Gavin Booth
Edinburgh

The Rear-Engined Double-Decker

The double-deck bus has always been regarded as a peculiarly British animal. True, there are some countries that have dabbled with double-deckers at various times, and others, usually in the Far East, that have discovered the advantages of two decks to move large numbers of people, but the British double-deck population of just under 25,000 is easily the biggest in the world.

Today's typical double-decker is a rear-engined vehicle, in fact nine out of every 10 are to this layout. Yet only 20 years ago nine out of 10 double-deckers were front-engined.

The apparent success of the rear-engined models in reversing this ratio masks a number of other factors which led British bus operators to change their buying habits.

The year 1950 was a watershed for single-deck buses. After years of buying buses with front-mounted engines, the introduction of underfloor-engined chassis prompted among major operators a very rapid switch to the new designs. The mid-mounted engine was conveniently tucked away out of sight under the floor, releasing more space for seated passengers — up to a total of 45; the front axle was set back allowing entrances at the extreme front under the driver's control; bodybuilders had a new freedom to build bodies that looked very modern in comparison to the more traditional designs of the time.

Operators were glad to have the extra seating capacity in the early 1950s, a time when the postwar travel boom was past its peak, but still required high-capacity buses.

Double-deck progress, by comparison, was evolutionary. Following London Transport's lead bigger engines were popular, set to work at much less than maximum power, and the driver's job was eased with synchromesh or preselective gearboxes on several models, instead of the awkward constant-mesh boxes still favoured by some manufacturers. Increasingly, air brakes were offered in place of vacuum brakes. AEC did develop a double-deck version of its underfloor-engined Regal Mk IV chassis, the Regent Mk IV, but it was not progressed with.

Leyland was at this time working on a concept that would change all that: a rear-engined double-decker. The rear-engined layout was not unknown in other countries, notably the United States, and Leyland and Midland Red had each produced experimental single-deckers in the 1930s and 1940s. Foden, essentially a truck builder, dabbled in the bus market in the late 1940s/early 1950s, and produced a rear-engined single-deck chassis in 1950 that was really a coach model. It has been suggested that had this been a *double*-decker it could well have hit the jackpot, but as a single-decker it was far from successful.

Interestingly, the Leyland experiments were carried out involving buses of traditional layout. They had the driver sitting over the front axle, and rear entrances with the engine actually mounted to the rear of the platform. This was possible because Leyland chose to use its O.350 unit, a small turbocharged 5.7-litre engine, rather than the big 9.8-litre O.600 engine of its contemporary Titan PD2 front-engined double-deck range.

Changes in the legislation governing vehicle dimensions meant that double-deckers could be up to 9.14m (30ft) long from July 1956, and this encouraged Leyland to redesign its rear-engined model with a set-back front axle, permitting a true front entrance, and the O.600 engine was specified, sitting transversely across the extreme rear of the chassis.

The resulting bus appeared later in 1956 and caused a sensation. Named Atlantean, it was a low-height integral bus — it had no chassis as such, and the body contributed to the overall structural strength. Bodybuilders Metro-Cammell Weymann (MCW) had worked with Leyland on the Atlantean as they had done previously on the Olympic, an integral single-deck bus.

At a stroke, Leyland had set the style for double-deck buses for the next few decades. And Leyland was not at the time the giant it later became. In 1956 it was still a rather solid, traditional Lancashire firm and there was little hint of the ambitious empire-building that was to follow in the 1960s. True, it had worked hard from the mid-1920s to establish itself as one of the top half-dozen bus builders in Britain, and had taken over Albion in 1951, but the Atlantean was an ambitious project.

The main competition for Leyland's mainstream double-deck model, the Titan, came from three sources — AEC, Daimler and Guy. AEC, probably its fiercest rival, was soundly based on London Transport business, with a sizeable export market; it had in 1948 expanded its influence with the purchase of two rival chassis builders,

Far left:
A scene typical of many British cities — rear-engined double-deckers awaiting their passengers. The first and last buses are Plymouth Leyland Atlantean AN68B/1R with East Lancs bodies, and the second a Roe-bodied Atlantean AN68A/1R from the same fleet, all typical municipal buses. The third bus is a Western National Bristol VRT with Eastern Coach Works body, representing the mainstay of many NBC fleets. M. Fowler

Left:
The body layout of rear-engined buses was in some ways anticipated by AEC's side-engined Q double-decker of the 1930s. On this model the engine was mounted behind the front axle, on the offside. This was London Transport Q2 of 1934 with 56-seat Metro-Cammell body, with the entrance ahead of the front axle, although without doors. The rear-ascending staircase behind the driver also became familiar a quarter of a century later on the first Atlanteans. Only 29 AEC Q double-deckers were built, including five trolleybuses and a six-wheel motor bus, but the Q proved more successful in single-deck form. London Transport

Crossley and Maudslay, and two principal bodybuilders, Park Royal and Roe. Daimler chassis were a popular choice with many municipal operators, and had been since the early 1930s when a decision was taken to standardise on chassis with preselective gearboxes. Guy had risen to prominence during World War 2 when it became the major supplier of utility double-deck chassis, and many operators stayed loyal in the postwar period.

Other double-deck chassis were on the market in 1956, at least in theory, from Atkinson and Dennis, and for nationalised operators there were Bristols. Like its sister company Eastern Coach Works (ECW), Bristol was an offshoot of a bus-operating undertaking and from 1948 built solely for nationalised fleets. The nationalised operators fell into two main camps: those that *could* buy Bristols as well as anything else, like London Transport and the Scottish Bus Group, and those that had little, if any, choice — the Tilling group companies.

The nationalised sector was a significant one, and an attractive one for bus builders, but a difficult one to break into. The Tilling companies were off-limits, and London Transport was firmly wedded to AEC and its standard postwar double-deck model, the RT. The Scottish companies had strong leanings towards Leylands and AECs, but Bristols were beginning to infiltrate some of the fleets.

The other major group was British Electric Traction (BET) with companies throughout England and Wales, often former tramway operators in the most densely-populated areas. BET had its favoured suppliers, notably AEC and Leyland, though its vehicle-buying policies were less rigid than Tilling's.

Just under 100 municipal operators represented an important group of potential customers; a few still ran trams in 1956, a larger number trolleybuses. But by far the majority of municipal vehicles were motorbuses, and double-deckers at that.

For Leyland's Atlantean, the municipals and the BET companies were the prime prospects, and the prototype bus was inspected by several major fleets. Feedback from operators resulted in changes to the specification. In production form in 1958 it emerged as a separate chassis; the integral concept was abandoned, partly to give operators a choice of bodybuilders, and the low-height requirement was dropped.

For years the quest for the perfect low-height bus occupied the manufacturers. Leyland had pioneered the lowbridge bus in 1927 with its original Titan TD1; this achieved an overall height of 3.96m (13ft) with a sunken offside gangway on the upper deck. Buses were built to this layout for the next 40 years, but a more satisfactory solution was needed. Bristol and ECW successfully developed the Lodekka in 1949, which used a drop-centre rear axle to lower the overall height to 4.06m (13ft 4in), with normal seating on both decks. This model was only sold to nationalised fleets, and other builders followed with similar low-height models designed to appeal to other sectors. In spite of the apparent desire for low-height buses, only the Lodekka was successful, no doubt due to a combination of its captive market and the fact that it was in production in the early 1950s. The others came later — going into production in the late 1950s/early 1960s — but by that time alternatives were available.

Leyland did not abandon the lowbridge market with its Atlantean chassis. While the normal-height version at approximately 4.42m (14ft 6in) was the main model, MCW produced a semi-lowbridge body with the normal upper deck layout for the forward rows of seats, and a raised platform with four-across seating for the rear four rows with access from a short nearside gangway. This was an awkward layout and appealed only to a few customers.

The first Atlanteans entered service late in 1958, and production was slow to get into full swing. By the end of 1960 only 633 Atlanteans were in service — 516 with BET fleets, 112 with municipals and five with independents.

Then Daimler joined the fray in 1960 with the Fleetline, a model that had two distinct advantages for many operators: a Gardner engine and a proper low-height capability. The Gardner engine was a popular choice with many operators, and was specified for most Daimler and Guy double-deckers. The low height was achieved with a drop-centre rear axle and meant that the same chassis could be used for either genuine low-height or normal-height bodies.

Fleetlines were initially slow to enter service, but by 1963 had almost reached Atlantean levels and in 1964 outsold the Leyland model. At this time front-engined double-deckers were still entering service in greater numbers than the rear-engined models, though this was in part due to the influence of London Transport and the Tilling group, with the Routemaster and Lodekka models. Remove them from the equation and the rear-engined designs accounted for nearly 60% of deliveries to the other sectors of the market.

To complicate matters further, there was a clear shift to high-capacity single-deck buses in many fleets that had previously been double-deck dominated. This largely coincided with the introduction of a new breed of rear-engined single-deck models with lower floor heights which were thus more suitable for urban service. One-man operated double-deckers were not legalised until 1966, and in the meantime some sizeable fleets had gone over to single-deckers.

This change of direction was particularly noticeable among the municipal fleets. For many years less than one in every 10 municipal buses was single-deck, but by 1974 the figure was two of every 10 — a significant increase. Some operators returned to double-deckers, but others stayed with single-deckers. London Transport was a surprising convert, placing no fewer than 1,365 single-deckers in service between 1966 and 1972, but then reverting to double-deckers in a big way.

With a wider double-deck choice in the 1960s it would be wrong to assume that operators stuck faithfully to a preferred design. Analysis of the period up to 1968, when major changes in the industry affected buying policies, shows that many operators were anxious to exercise their freedom of choice. With 13 double-deck models (only two rear-engined) available for most of the 1960s, the patterns of purchase are of particular interest.

Among the municipalities some stuck firmly to front-engined designs. These were usually the smaller undertakings, often in the northwest of England. A growing number were 'converted' during the 1960s, although it was notable that 'Leyland' fleets did not always choose the Atlantean. On the other hand some municipal operators actually returned to front-engined chassis after experience with early Atlanteans.

Of the larger municipal fleets, some like Birmingham, Liverpool, Newcastle, Plymouth and Portsmouth decided at an early stage to standardise on one model. Others, like Bolton, Coventry and Glasgow, eventually settled down with a standard model, while some kept their options open and took an amazing variety of types. Leeds, Leicester, Manchester, Nottingham, Salford and Sheffield were among the fleets that rang the changes in the 1960s.

Things were rather more orderly among the BET fleets at the time. By the end of the decade — and, indeed, the end of BET as a major force in the British bus industry — most fleets has gone over to rear-engined models. Only Aldershot & District and South Wales stuck to front-engined designs.

Interestingly, some of the early Atlantean users in the BET group had switched to Fleetlines: Maidstone & District, Potteries and Trent all deserted Leyland in their search for a better low-height bus.

Scottish Bus Group (SBG) fleets tended to shop around in the 1960s mixing Leyland Titans, Albion Lowlanders and Bristol Lodekkas before eventually plumping for the Fleetline as the main double-deck model. SBG never bought any new Atlanteans, a consequence of the Group's chronic low bridge problem.

Leyland did produce a 'real' low-height Atlantean in 1964, the PDR1/2 model, but for most operators with this requirement the Fleetline was the main choice.

The Tilling group companies had of course been restricted to Bristol/ECW products since 1948, and likewise Bristol/ECW products were restricted to nationalised fleets. During the 1960s Leyland was expanding its empire and its influence with the purchase of AEC (1962), Standard-Triumph (1961) and Rover (1967). With the new Leyland Motor Corporation now controlling on the bus side AEC, Albion, Leyland, Park Royal and Roe, further expansion seemed inevitable. This came with a deal in 1965, a share exchange between Leyland and the Transport Holding Company (THC). Leyland's new share in Bristol and ECW brought these products back on to the open market and shortly afterwards a new rear-engined double-deck chassis appeared, the Bristol VRL.

Unlike the Atlantean and Fleetline the VRL had its engine mounted longitudi-

Below:
Until Leyland Atlanteans became familiar, some operators chose 30ft front-engined buses with forward entrance bodywork, like this rather drab Yorkshire Woollen District AEC Regent V with MCW Orion bodywork.
MCW

Right:
The bus that changed it all: prototype Leyland Low-loader of 1951, STF 90, with Saunders-Roe bodywork. The O.350 engine can just be seen on the rear platform, and the driver over the front axle with apparently wasted space to his left where the engine would normally be. The bus was bought by Lloyds of Nuneaton, and used between 1958 and 1961. T. W. Moore

Bottom:
Maidstone & District was one of the early Leyland Atlantean customers who switched to Daimler Fleetlines when they came on to the market, to provide a proper low-height layout. This 1963 Fleetline, one of 35 with Northern Counties bodywork, was still in service at Sevenoaks 14 years later.
S. J. Butler

nally on the rear offside. In this form only two prototypes and 30 coaches were built for the home market, and Bristol, encouraged by potential customers, concentrated on developing a transverse engined equivalent, the VRT, which first appeared in 1968.

The fortunes of Daimler and Guy had been mixed and the companies had sold out to Jaguar Cars — Daimler in 1960 and the bankrupt Guy in 1961. Jaguar merged with the British Motor Corporation in 1966 to form British Motor Holdings (BMH), and in 1968 Leyland and BMH merged to form a new giant, the British Leyland Motor Corporation. This effectively brought all of Britain's remaining builders of full-size buses under Leyland control; the repercussions would be felt for many years.

The whole bus industry was undergoing major changes in the late 1960s. On the operating side BET had sold out to THC, and a new organisation, the National Bus Company (NBC) was formed to control them.

No fewer than 20 municipal operators, including giants like Birmingham, Liverpool and Manchester, would disappear into four new Passenger Transport Executives (PTEs), new bodies with transport responsibilities for an entire conurbation area. And London Transport's sprawling area was divided into two, with London Country, a new NBC fleet, assuming control of the ring of outer areas.

One-man operation of double-deckers became legal in 1966, and this tipped the scales in favour of the rear-engined designs, where the set-back front axle permitted easier cash-collecting and ticket-issuing arrangements. By 1968, 85% of new double-deckers were rear-engined; a year later the figure was 98%, by 1970 victory was complete.

The trend away from front-engined designs was hastened by several factors. The last AEC Routemasters and Bristol Lodekkas were built in 1968, so the two big-selling operator-designed models no longer unbalanced the figures; the desire for one-man double-deckers was another factor, as were Leyland's plans for rationalising its complex range; and it was

Left:
One of the earliest production Daimler Fleetlines was this 1961 bus for the Scottish independent A1 Service, and its Northern Counties body introduced a neater rear outline, disguising the prominent bustle of the engine compartment. Roy Marshall

known that a scheme of Bus Grants was to be introduced by government to encourage purchases of particular types of vehicle and speed fleet renewal.

The new forces in the industry, NBC and the PTEs, represented massive purchasing power and clearly could — and did — influence the bus market. For both NBC and the PTEs vehicle standardisation had obvious attractions. NBC's total fleet of 16,000 buses, and another 6,000 between the four PTEs, represented over 30% of the public sector, and the later creation of a further three PTEs pushed this total up to over 50% by 1976.

NBC inherited a mixture of fleets. The old Tilling fleets with their Bristol/ECW connection were more orderly; the BET group had a more catholic view on vehicle purchases and contained a staggering collection of chassis and body types. The PTEs were just as bad.

Clearly, standards were needed, and NBC's first move was to create a partnership with British Leyland to design and build a new integral single-deck bus, the Leyland National. For double-deckers it chose the Bristol VRT, but other problems forced NBC to dual-source in 1974 and some fleets received Atlanteans.

The PTEs pursued their individual lines. Merseyside chose Atlanteans, Fleetlines and VRTs; SELNEC chose Atlanteans and Fleetlines; Tyneside stuck to Atlanteans; and West Midlands to Fleetlines and VRTs.

Leyland's monopoly of chassis supply was causing concern in some areas. The lack of real choice was aggravated by the economic and labour problems of the early 1970s which culminated in the three-day week in the winter of 1973/74. Chassis delivery began to slip badly and this had a knock-on effect with body builders that took some years to rectify.

The Fleetline was particularly badly hit by the industrial situation and by specific factors like the 1973 shift of production from Coventry to Leyland and a strike at Gardner that delayed engine supplies. Some operators were still awaiting 1973 Fleetline deliveries in 1976 and this situation was complicated by London Transport's decision to standardise on the model, which meant that for several years nearly half of Fleetline production was for the capital; in 1974/75 the figure reached over 60%.

The problems of monopoly and production delays prompted other builders to look closely at the market. The last non-Leyland group double-deck model in production had been the Dennis Loline in 1967 and so the arrival of two new double-deckers in 1973 caused great interest.

The Metropolitan represented an interesting liaison between MCW, the Birmingham-based bodybuilder, and the Swedish manufacturer Scania. It was in essence a double-deck version of the integrally-constructed Metro-Scania city bus that had been available in Britain since 1969. It was rear-engined.

The Ailsa broke new ground as it featured a *front* engine and a set-back front axle. Guy had produced the similar Wulfrunian model between 1959 and 1965 without great success, but the Ailsa, developed by Scottish-based Volvo truck importers, used a small turbocharged engine that occupied less space at the front than the Wulfrunian's hefty 6LX unit.

Frustrated bus operators ordered the new models to maintain deliveries and, one suspects, to give Leyland a fright. By 1975 the Metropolitan had 10% of the double-deck market, mainly PTEs, but also municipalities like Hull and Leicester. In 1978 production was being phased out, but over the five years 659 had been built for British fleets, with substantial batches for London Transport and Tyne & Wear PTE.

The Ailsa appealed initially to Scottish operators with SBG fleets, Greater Glasgow PTE and Tayside as the main customers. Some English PTEs chose Ailsas, partly as a stopgap until Fleetline production was back to normal: South Yorkshire and West Midlands received batches in this way. The Ailsa had a longer production run than the Metropolitan, but totals sold to British operators were little more than 700-plus.

In spite of the delays double-deck deliveries stayed at a high level during the 1970s, averaging just over 1,900 each year in the second half of the decade. And a growing list of models was seeking out the business.

Leyland had announced its intention to replace its three double-deck models with a new advanced specification vehicle and the Fleetline would be the first to go. This alerted other builders, for the Fleetline had been a consistently good seller with roundly half the double-deck market in the early 1970s.

The essential ingredients were seen to be the Gardner engine and a low-height capability, and both Dennis and Foden entered the fray in 1977 with models meeting this broad specification. Dennis produced the Dominator, and Foden and bodybuilder Northern Counties the Foden-NC. Although the Foden never got beyond the prototype stage, the Dennis managed to pick up a number of municipal Fleetline customers and found its most enthusiastic supporter in South Yorkshire PTE.

Leyland's advanced double-decker materialised as the Titan in 1978 but production difficulties and other uncertainties discouraged many potential customers and it eventually settled down as a London model. Leyland quickly learned that not all operators wished this degree of sophistication and revised its model-replacement plans. The Atlantean in its upgraded AN68 form from 1972 was still selling well — an average of over 600 a year between 1972 and 1981, with roundly 30% of the market.

The surprising performer for Leyland at this time was the Bristol VRT which was suddenly catapulted into prominence in the mid-1970s, mainly supplying NBC fleets. Its best-ever year was 1980, when over 600 were supplied and the VRT actually outsold all other models.

But the ageing Atlantean and VRT could only hold off the competition for a short time and a new model was needed, particularly when MCW's Metrobus burst on to the market in 1978 and successfully picked up some significant orders — notably from London Transport and West Midlands PTE.

Although London was buying its double-deckers off-the-peg, it still craved a return to the days of bespoke London models. The last LT-designed bus had been the classic Routemaster and although there had been a rear-engined Routemaster prototype developed in 1966, this was a victim of Leyland's model rationalisation and was stillborn. In the 1970s LT's engineers were working on a new model, coded XRM, which would be built by manufacturers to London designs. A four-year development programme was started in 1975, but by 1980 the project had been shelved. Had the XRM been built it would have had a side-mounted engine and one of the options was a four-axle design, with twin steering axles.

The peak years for double-deck deliveries in Britain were between 1975 and 1981; after this the number of new vehicles dropped significantly. Unfortunately for Leyland its new Atlantean/VRT replacement, the Olympian, came in just at the tail of this. Since that time it has been virtually a two-horse race.

Above:
Some fleets continued to buy both front-engined and rear-engined buses, and A1 Service of Ardrossan, as a co-operative organisation, was subject to the whims of the individual owners. At Kilmarnock in 1974, a 1964 AEC Renown/Park Royal and a Daimler Fleetline/Alexander just two years newer; both had seats for 75 passengers.
Malcolm Keeley

Right:
The SBG companies had bought the Bristol/ECW Lodekka in large numbers, and were early customers for the replacement VRT model. This Central SMT example was new in 1969, but within a few years all SBG VRTs had been swapped with NBC companies for Lodekkas. This bus ended up with Lincolnshire. Roy Marshall

Atlantean was phased out in 1984, Fleetline and VRT in 1982, and Titan in 1984. The Ailsa was replaced by the Volvo Citybus in 1983/84. The Metrobus and Olympian have been virtually neck-and-neck since 1982 with London orders holding the key to success. Metrobus and Titan had shared London's business since 1978, with Olympian successfully winning the 1986 London order.

Observers had been predicting a severe drop in double-deck bus orders in the 1980s with the end of the Bus Grants scheme seen as a primary factor. But 1986 brought new uncertainties to the whole industry, resulting in drastically cut orders to help reduce costs, large-scale use of minibuses, and a thriving second-hand market. Deregulation, the breaking up of the Metropolitan Counties, and the privatisation of NBC — all of these factors created a mood of unease which was reflected in low delivery levels.

Recent interest in second-hand double-deckers has rather distorted the overall market situation. London Transport started a trend when it began premature withdrawal of its big Fleetline class. From 1979, barely months after deliveries had been completed, the former London DM and DMS class buses started to appear in a wide range of fleets — PTEs, municipals, NBC, SBG and independents, often the very fleets that suffered the frustration of delayed Fleetline delivery in the 1970s.

Further second-hand vehicles came on to the market in 1986 when several of the PTEs found it necessary to shed buses in preparation for their re-emergence as limited companies. Greater Manchester, Merseyside, South Yorkshire, Strathclyde and West Yorkshire all disposed of buses in quantity, which were eagerly snapped up by other operators. This in turn further depressed the new bus market as it plunged lower with little immediate sign of recovery.

The one bright spot in the 1980s has been a resurgence of interest in double-deck coaches. British operators, notably

Ribble, had specified several generations of double-deck coach, the last being the 11m (36ft) Bristol VRLs in the late 1960s. On the continent of Europe, although double-deckers were little used for bus duties, there was a growing interest for sightseeing work.

Auwarter, the West German builders of the Neoplan range, had considerable expertise in building three-axle luxury vehicles and sold a batch to Trathens of Yelverton in 1981 for a London-Plymouth service. These have been followed by similar Neoplan Skyliners for fleets like Stagecoach and Yelloway, and by other models from European manufacturers like Kassbohrer (Setra) and Van Hool. British manufacturers entered this market with some trepidation: Leyland produced a long-wheelbase Olympian with ECW body for NBC fleets; Plaxtons' 4000 body has been built on Neoplan and Scania underframes in full double-deck form; and MCW produced the three-axle Metroliner in full double-deck form in 1982, followed by the 4m (13ft 1in) high 400GT model in 1986. In addition, British bodybuilders, notably Alexander and East Lancs, have built double-deck luxury coach bodies on Leyland Olympian and Volvo Citybus chassis.

A compromise, in true British fashion, has been the increased trend to fit coach-type seating in what are essentially standard service bus body shells, externally distinguished only by brighter liveries. There was nothing particularly new about this. For some years a small proportion of double-deck deliveries were to a higher specification, but during the 1980s the idea really caught on. It started in earnest in 1984 when a number of NBC and municipal fleets bought vehicles to this specification. These allowed a more flexible role, as local buses, longer-distance vehicles and for private hire duties. Since that time SBG, independents, and PTEs and their successors have followed suit.

The only real challenge to the double-decker's supremacy as a people-mover has been the articulated bus. Essentially a European concept, where height clearances can be a problem, the idea of carrying up to 180 passengers — seated and standing — in a long single-deck vehicle had never seemed to appeal in Britain. The double-decker, with roughly 75 seats, was usually seen as the preferred option. Even when larger capacities were available, on 10m (32ft 9in) double-deckers for instance, operators were reluctant to incur the extra cost and weight penalties. With possible seated capacities of up to 86, the longer double-deckers have only found favour with a small number of undertakings; Lothian has been the most notable recent convert. Others have dabbled with longer buses, reverting to the more common length of 9.5-9.6m (31ft 2in-31ft 6in). Where rigid single-deckers like the Leyland National offered capacities that rivalled those on double-deckers (77-52 plus 25 standing), British operators preferred to stick to layouts providing the maximum seating capacity.

Several operators, notably South Yorkshire PTE, lobbied for articulated buses in the late 1970s, and in the 1980 Transport Act these were legalised in Britain. South Yorkshire bought 10 articulated Leyland-DABs and MANs in 1979/80, but union problems forced their withdrawal in 1981. Further interest was limited — 10 were bought for airside use by British Airways and Luton Airport — and it seemed the concept was dead in Britain until 1985 when South Yorkshire rekindled its interest with 13 more Leyland-DABs, including three to coach specification.

It would be unrealistic to forecast a healthy future for the articulated bus in Britain, at a time when the health of that traditional urban mainstay, the double-decker, is suffering from a combination of external factors that threaten the survival of a thriving and competitive manufacturing industry. For its part, the bus operating industry is unlikely to return to its expansive buying policies of the early 1970s until the market settles sufficiently. The double-decker is far from dead, but if the recent fall in buying trends continued the logical outcome would be *no* new double-deckers entering service after only 16 years, and with an average life of 12-15 years, Britain's present total fleet of 25,000 double-deckers would quickly decline. Common sense tells us that this will not happen, but it is an indication of the gravity of the situation.

It seems most likely that the record buying years of 1975-81, when over 14,000 new double-deckers entered service, will be reflected in replacement requirements in the late 1980s/early 1990s. That, at any rate, is what the manufacturers hope.

Below:
A few operators have extended the lives of their older rear-engined chassis by rebodying them. Southend has rebodied Fleetlines, and these Cleveland Transit Atlanteans were rebodied by Northern Counties in 1986.
S. J. Butler

The First Generation

1 Leyland Atlantean PDR series

PDR1/1, PDR1/2
Wheelbase: 4.95m (16ft 3in)
Engine: Leyland O.600 9.8-litre naturally-aspirated six-cylinder diesel
Rating: 130bhp @ 1,800rpm
Gearbox: Air-shift Pneumocyclic, semi-automatic
Retarder: No
Brakes: Diaphragm air brakes
Steering gear: Cam-and-double-roller
Rear axle: Single reduction (PDR1/2: stepped double reduction)
Suspension: Semi-elliptic springs

PDR1A/1, PDR1/3, PDR2/1
Wheelbase: 4.95m (16ft 3in) (PDR2/1: 5.64m [18ft 6in])
Engine: Leyland O.600 9.8-litre naturally-aspirated six-cylinder diesel
Rating: 130bhp @ 1,800rpm
Gearbox: Air-shift Pneumocyclic, semi-automatic
Retarder: No
Brakes: Dual line split braking system
Steering gear: Cam-and-double-roller
Rear axle: Single reduction (PDR1/3: fully floating stepped double reduction)
Suspension: Semi-elliptic laminated leaf type
Options: Leyland 680 engine (11.1-litre, developing 153bhp @ 1,750rpm)
Fully-automatic Pneumocyclic gearbox
Power-assisted steering

The Model

Leyland Motors Ltd was one of the top five double-deck bus manufacturers in Britain, along with AEC, Bristol, Daimler and Guy. It had regular customers and a large slice of the market with its front-engined Titan range of chassis. The first Titan had been the TD1 model of 1927, and in 1956 the current model was the PD2, introduced in 1947 with the new 9.8-litre O.600 Leyland engine and synchromesh gearbox. Unlike other builders, Leyland only fitted its own engines, but there was a wide range of model options depending on chassis width, preference for an exposed radiator or full-width front, vacuum or air brakes, and gearbox choice; the synchromesh unit was most popular, but London Transport, and to a much lesser degree Leeds City Transport, had specified PD2s with preselective gearboxes. The Pneumocyclic gearbox, which could have semi-automatic or fully-automatic control, was introduced as a further option in 1954.

In 1956 the Construction & Use regulations were relaxed to permit 9.14m (30ft) long double-deckers and Leyland added the longer-wheelbase PD3 variants to its Titan model list.

At the same time, Leyland had been experimenting with different engines and different engine positions. In 1952-54 it had built two prototype rear-engined

Above right:
The second Leyland Low-loader prototype, XTC 684, looked rather more conventional than STF 90, and still echoed the looks of front-engined buses. Bodywork was by MCW. After service with independents, it was sold for preservation. Stewart J. Brown

Right:
The new shape of rear-engined double-deckers was set by the layout of the production Leyland Atlantean PDR1/1 chassis, which allowed bodies to be more box-like. This was one of the first Atlanteans in service, Glasgow Corporation LA1 of 1958, with 78-seat Alexander body. It is now preserved. Stewart J. Brown

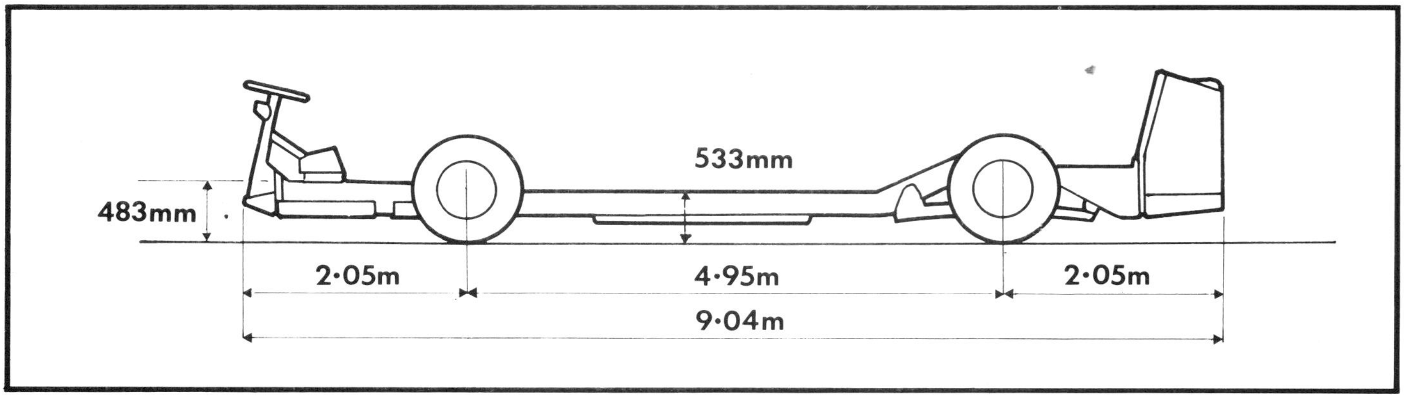

double-deckers, the first ever in Britain, with small engines (Leyland's Comet O.350 engine, turbocharged) on the rear platform. Several operators evaluated these as part of the development programme.

Then in 1956 Leyland shook the bus world with the Atlantean, a totally new concept in double-deckers. It was 9.14m (30ft) long and had a set-back front axle with an entrance right by the driver in the manner of most contemporary single-deck buses. The engine was the bigger O.600, mounted transversely across the rear wall, and Pneumocyclic transmission was fitted. The Atlantean was conceived as a complete bus only 4.04m (13ft 3in) high, and with integrally-constructed bodywork by MCW with seats for 78.

The low height was an attempt to produce a single model to suit all conditions, and while the integral construction made for structural rigidity and allowed height to be kept down, British operators were wary of integrals. A few underfloor-engined single-deck models had been introduced as integrals, but operators had shown a clear preference for the British body-on-chassis concept.

The 1956 Atlantean prototype was extensively tested and in 1958 the Atlantean reappeared in production form. Now it was a separate chassis, coded PDR1/1, and the low-height problem was pushed into the background. Operators requiring low-height vehicles could specify bodywork that was a variation on the lowbridge side-gangway layout. The rear part of the upper saloon seating was raised to compensate for rear axle clearance on the

Above right:
Manchester Corporation placed a cautious order with Leyland for 10 Atlanteans which entered service in 1959. The MCW 77-seat bodywork was typical of many early Atlanteans. Manchester and its PTE successors were to become the biggest customers for the Atlantean, and deliveries only ceased in 1984. R. L. Wilson

Right:
Ribble took early semi-lowheight Atlanteans, some of which enjoyed surprisingly long lives. This 1960 example with Weymann 72-seat body illustrates the shallower lower deck windows and flatter roof profile compared with the normal-height Manchester bus. M. Fowler

lower deck. In practice, full-height buses were more popular.

A true low-height model appeared in 1964, the PDR1/2, which achieved this in the same way as the new rival model, the Daimler Fleetline: it used the same drop-centre rear axle as Leyland's front-engined Albion Lowlander, and the Daimler direct-selection epicyclic gearbox with concentric drive, as used in the Fleetline, was fitted in place of the normal Pneumocyclic unit.

In 1966 Leyland produced a longer-wheelbase Atlantean, model PDR2/1, suitable for bodies up to 10m (32ft 9in) long. Some operators went for the longer buses, but most reverted to 9.5m (31ft 2in) as a standard length. In 1964 the PDR1/2 was replaced by a new low-height Atlantean variant, the PDR1/3. This had the same drop centre rear axle, but the transmission was changed and the rationalised Pneumocyclic gearbox fitted.

This improved gearbox was also fitted to the main Atlantean model in 1967, which was redesignated PDR1A/1.

By the late 1960s Leyland's early domination of the market was waning. During that decade it had sold an average of more than 380 Atlantean each year to British operators; Daimler's average for the Fleetline during the period 1962-66 was only 338. But in 1964 Fleetline outsold Atlantean for the first time and would continue to do so virtually every year until 1978.

If the Atlantean was to survive, it had to be drastically updated. So in 1971 the last PDR series Atlanteans entered service with British operators. Some of the last deliveries were PDR1A/1 Specials, to all intents an interim model incorporating some of the features of the replacement. These went to London Country, Maidstone & District, Merseyside PTE and Northern General.

The Market

Of the first four Atlantean PDR1/1s, built in 1958, two were for municipal operators and two for BET group fleets. These sectors became the main customers in the

Left:
The independent Laurie of Hamilton (Chieftain) bought Scotland's second Atlantean, in 1960. It had MCW 77-seat bodywork, and was joined by a second bus in 1961. Both passed briefly to Central SMT with the Laurie business in 1961. Roy Marshall

Below:
Leicester City Transport went through a period of apparent indecision in the 1960s. After three of these PDR1/1 Atlanteans with MCW 77-seat bodywork were delivered in 1963 it bought batches of Leyland Titan PD3s, AEC Renowns and more Atlanteans, before settling briefly on the MCW Metropolitan in the 1970s. Behind the Leicester bus is one of Midland Red's many Alexander-bodied Daimler Fleetlines, buses that marked an end to the company's long line of in-house BMMO double-deck models. Stewart J. Brown

1960s, with a handful for independents and an experimental batch for London Transport the only other sales.

Many municipal operators adopted a cautious approach to the new breed and took one for evaluation: Belfast, Birmingham, Glasgow, Liverpool and Walsall fell into this category. Others took small batches — Chesterfield, Great Yarmouth, Hull, Manchester, Newcastle — while only Sheffield (44), Wallasey (20) and Plymouth (18) really committed themselves in the 1958-60 period. By the end of 1960, 112 Atlanteans were in service with British municipalities.

The BET group companies were more adventurous. By the end of 1960 there were 516 Atlanteans in service, with big fleets at Ribble (95), Maidstone & District (80), Potteries (75), Trent (54) and Devon General (40).

Traditional Leyland customers were clearly most likely to buy Atlanteans, but with a greater market choice, operators were inclined to shop around and some Atlanteans joined well-mixed fleets.

During the 1960s the pattern changed. While some operators stuck firmly with the Atlantean, others turned again to front-engined designs. There was another group still that stayed unwaveringly with front-engined designs.

On the municipal side, Hull, Newcastle, Plymouth, Portsmouth and Wallasey stayed faithful to the Atlantean; Birmingham switched to Fleetlines; Birkenhead, Bury, Chesterfield, Leicester, Lincoln, Nottingham, Salford, Sheffield and Walsall all went back to front-engined models, albeit briefly.

But there was also the growing list of converts, like Ashton, Blackburn, Bolton, Colchester, Edinburgh, Glasgow, Ipswich, Liverpool, Maidstone, Newport, Oldham, Southampton, Stockton, TRTB and Wigan, all of whom changed from front-engined designs during the 1960s.

Top left:
BET group fleets were enthusiastic Atlantean users from the start, and this Devon General bus was a 1959 delivery, with MCW 76-seat bodywork. Devon General then reverted to front-engined models for a while, like the new AEC Regent seen to the left of the Atlantean.
Roy Marshall

Above left:
Birmingham City Transport tried 10 Atlantean PDR1/1 with 76-seat MCW bodies in 1961, but was unmoved by the model's appeal. The undertaking became an enthusiastic Fleetline user instead. One of the Birmingham buses is seen in 1972 in West Midlands PTE livery, followed by one of Walsall's unusual short-length Fleetlines. Roy Marshall

Left:
Another early independent Atlantean PDR1/1, delivered to Bamber Bridge Motor Services in 1963, with low-height Weymann 72-seat body. It passed with the Bamber Bridge business to Ribble in 1967, joining similar buses like the example illustrated earlier.
Roy Marshall

Some operators bought Atlanteans *and* Fleetlines: Aberdeen, Bournemouth, Bradford, Coventry, Great Yarmouth; whilst others apparently bought anything. During the period 1963-65 Leeds bought Atlanteans and Fleetlines as well as front-engined models from AEC, Daimler and Leyland; and over the 1962-65 period Leicester bought Atlanteans and front-engined Leyland Titan PD3s and AEC Bridgemasters and Renowns.

Top:
Although Maidstone Corporation was a good Atlantean customer, it later sold its double-deck fleet in favour of lighter-weight single-deck Bedfords. This 1965 PDR1/1 had bodywork by the Wigan builder Massey. Note the overhead trolleybus wires; Maidstone replaced its last trolleybuses in 1967.
M. Fowler

Right:
Stockton Corporation bought a batch of these Atlantean PDR1/1 with Park Royal 74-seat bodies in 1964. Note the unusual selection of ventilators and opening windows, and the faired-in engine compartment. R. L. Wilson

BET group companies were apparently equally uncertain during the 1960s. Some fleets stuck to Atlanteans, often with a scattering of front-engined chassis: Devon General, East Midland, Northern General, Ribble, Western Welsh and Yorkshire Traction. Others, including some of the early Atlantean customers, changed horses and turned to Daimler's Fleetline: Maidstone & District, Potteries and Trent were no doubt attracted by Fleetline's 'proper' low-height arrangement.

London Transport had always been an important customer for Leyland, particularly after Leyland and AEC merged in 1962. London's standard model had been the Routemaster, supplied in substantial numbers from 1959 to 1968, but LT was looking at alternative designs and bought an experimental batch of 50 Atlanteans in 1965. These were to be London's only Atlanteans and had short lives, being sold in 1973.

Independent operators, by their very nature, were not large Atlantean customers, but in the period to 1972 more than 70 entered service with independent fleets. The biggest customers in this sector were A1 Service (11), Fishwick (10), South Yorkshire (8), AA (6) and Severn (6).

When the PDR series Atlantean was replaced by the AN series in 1972, over 5,500 had been built for the home market. Of these over 2,000 were with municipalities, around 1,500 with PTEs and around 1,100 with NBC fleets, mostly ex-BET group companies.

Top right:
When London Transport bought 50 Atlantean PDR1/1 in 1965 the Stockton-style Park Royal body was specified. The London buses had 680 engines, and this one is seen in West Croydon operating as a one-man bus.
Stewart J. Brown

Above right:
Ribble took 10 of these PDR1/2 Atlanteans with low-height Alexander bodywork; the body style represents one of the earlier attempts to break away from the previous box-like shapes, with interesting use of curved glass and plastics. Stewart J. Brown

Right:
Another PDR1/2 with low-height body, a 1966 West Riding example. The Roe 76-seat bodywork had a suggestion of the Alexander body at the front end. West Riding was an independent company at that time, and had invested in a large and not entirely successful fleet of Guy Wulfrunian buses between 1959 and 1965. In 1967 West Riding sold out to the Transport Holding Company. Roy Marshall

Facing page, top:
The longer 10m Atlanteans were favoured by some operators, although most reverted to the shorter 9.4m length. This PDR2/1 of 1969 with 10m Park Royal two-door 79-seat body was one of three that were used by the Ayrshire co-operative A1 Service.
Roy Marshall

Facing page, bottom:
A PDR2/1 Atlantean chassis in the form that they were delivered to bodybuilders. Note the low frame at the front to provide a low entrance platform, and the straight rear axle, requiring a step or ramp in the lower saloon.
Leyland

A1
KILMARNOCK
A1 SERVICE
OCS 817H

2 Daimler Fleetline

CRG6

Wheelbase: 4.95m (16ft 3in)
Engine: Gardner 6LX 10.45-litre naturally-aspirated six-cylinder diesel
Rating: 150bhp @ 1,700rpm
Gearbox: Daimatic 4-speed semi-automatic, electro-pneumatic
Retarder: No
Brakes: Air pressure
Steering gear: Daimler worm and nut
Rear axle: Two-stage drop down reduction axle
Suspension: Semi-elliptic leaf springs
Options: Gardner 6LW 8.4-litre engine

FE30AGR

Wheelbase: 4.95m (16ft 3in)
Engine: Gardner 6LXB 10.45-litre naturally-aspirated six-cylinder diesel
Rating: 188bhp @ 1,850rpm
Gearbox: Daimatic 4-speed semi-automatic direct air-operated epicyclic
Retarder: No
Brakes: Air-operated dual-line split system
Steering gear: Daimler worm and nut, power assisted
Rear axle: Daimler two-stage drop centre reduction
Suspension: Overslung semi-elliptic leaf springs
Options: Leyland 680 engine (11.1-litre, developing 165bhp @ 1,900rpm) on FE30ALR
Fully-automatic 4-speed gearbox
Manual steering

The Model

Daimler's double-deck strength was in the municipal market, where the combination of the reliable, economic Gardner engine and preselective gearbox made its front-engined CV range a popular urban choice.

Leyland's sales success was more broadly based and its new Atlantean model was already proving popular with municipal and BET group fleets, even the awkward semi-lowbridge variant. Daimler apparently was considering developing a low-height *front*-engined model similar to AEC's 1956 Bridgemaster, but opted instead for a rear-engined low-height design — an astute move as it transpired.

The Fleetline prototypes were shown at the 1960 Commercial Motor Show and were broadly similar in layout to the Leyland Atlantean, but with a drop-centre rear axle to allow low-height bodies with normal seating on both decks. The prototypes were fitted with Daimler's own CD6 engine, a unit introduced in 1945, but most postwar Daimlers had Gardner engines, and the Gardner 6LX became the standard Fleetline engine, with a few operators choosing the lower-powered 6LW.

The first CRG6LX Fleetlines entered service in some quantity in 1962 and from the start Daimler attracted some interesting new customers. There were also some interesting model variations, like the short-length Fleetlines for Walsall Corporation and SHMD Board from 1962 and a 10m (32ft 9in) version from 1966.

At the same time Daimler was taking a fresh interest in the single-deck market with the Roadliner and the single-deck Fleetline. The Roadliner was a singularly unsuccessful chassis, due in no small part to the Cummins V6-200 engine, but the concept of a single-deck version of the Fleetline was more popular and some 360 were built for home-market customers, compared with 189 Roadliners.

Right:
The first completed Daimler Fleetline was 7000 HP, the demonstrator with MCW bodywork, which was sold to Tailby & George (Blue Bus Service) of Willington, but was lost in a depot fire in 1976. Roy Marshall

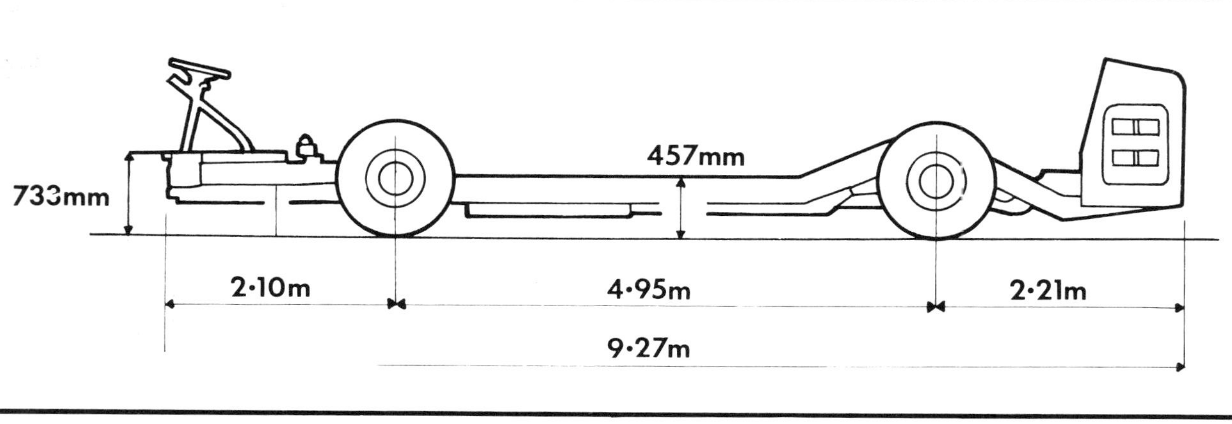

Improvements to the Fleetline were steadily made over the years and the first major change was the introduction of the Leyland 680 engine as an option in 1970, the CRL6 model, allowing Leyland to drop the less successful PDR1/3 Atlantean in favour of a more acceptable Leyland-engined low-height Fleetline.

The decision to switch Fleetline production to Leyland in 1973 caused severe production problems, aggravated by the industrial unrest of the time. The model actually became the *Leyland* Fleetline in 1974, redesignated FE30GR for the most popular Gardner-engined variant, nominally 9.14m (30ft), but more typically around 9.5m (31ft 2in). London Transport had been the major Fleetline customer in the 1970s and the last 400 of LT's 2,646 DM/DMS class buses had specially-quietened Leyland 690 engines (a turbo-charged version of the 680), and were known as B20s.

But the Fleetline was on its way out. Leyland was developing a replacement for the Fleetline, Bristol VRT and Leyland Atlantean, which materialised as the Leyland Olympian. Fleetline sales slowed down after 1978, and production ceased in 1980, although the last bodied buses were delivered in 1983, to Cleveland Transit.

The Market

Some of Daimler's traditional customers tried the Fleetline in its early years, but most orders were placed by undertakings with little or no recent Daimler experience. In the first five years of production nearly 1,000 Fleetlines were bought by municipalities, with particularly large orders placed by Belfast, Birmingham, Manchester, Middlesbrough, Nottingham, Sheffield and Walsall. The PTEs that succeeded some of these fleets continued to take Fleetlines; for West Midlands it was very much the main model, for the other English PTEs the Fleetline was bought along with other models.

Top right:
Lancashire United, then an independent company, bought various double-deck models in the 1960s — Dennis Loline, Guy Arab IV, Guy Arab V, a single Guy Wulfrunian, and batches of Daimler Fleetline CRG6LX like this 1962 example with Northern Counties 76-seat body. Front-engined Guys were bought until 1967, and Fleetlines only became the standard LUT model from 1970.
R. L. Wilson

Above right:
Sunderland Corporation bought Daimler Fleetline CRG6LX between 1962 and 1965 before changing to high-capacity rear-engined single-deck models. This Fleetline had Roe bodywork with peaked front and rear domes, an early effort to improve appearance. This was a 1965 example. Geoff Coxon

Right:
Like Sunderland, South Shields Corporation became a part of the Tyne & Wear PTE. The South Shields undertaking had bought front-engined Daimlers like the 1963 CCG6 on the left, before turning to Fleetlines in 1965/66, like 194 on the right, a 1965 Roe-bodied 76-seat one-door bus. John Burnett

The BET group companies had no Daimler tradition but the Fleetline changed this and appeared in a variety of fleets, often those requiring low-height buses. Maidstone & District, Midland Red, North Western and Potteries were the most enthusiastic early users and the biggest fleets built up by BET companies were by Midland Red (304), Trent (109) and Maidstone & District (105).

The Fleetline succeeded with Scottish Bus Group companies where Atlantean had made no impact. Over a 15-year period SBG took 640 Fleetlines. Independent operators bought over 200 Fleetlines, with Lancashire United taking 53, and A1 Service 37; most of the other big customers were also in Scotland — 12 for AA, 15 for

Top:
Walsall Corporation had unusual ideas about bus design. Between 1963 and 1969 it bought 99 short-length Fleetlines with Gardner 6LW engines, and with Northern Counties bodywork. This 1965 bus was later rebuilt to two-door layout, with a narrow door ahead of the front axle. T. W. Moore

Above right:
The SHMD Board was the only other operator to specify the Walsall-type short Fleetline. This 1968 example with 68-seat two-door Northern Counties body is seen after transfer to Greater Manchester PTE. Malcolm Keeley

Right:
West Midlands PTE became a sizeable Fleetline user, and bought over 1,200 buses over 11 years. This 1970 CRG6LX had 76-seat Park Royal bodywork, and is seen in Walsall in 1977. Malcolm Keeley

Graham, 14 for McGill. South Notts also received 14, including the two last chassis built in 1980, but delivered late in 1981.

But the biggest single customer was London Transport, which took eight in 1965 as part of an experiment and from 1970 received a further 2,646. London's inability to adapt to the 'off-the-peg' Fleetline is well known and the buses were sold out of service after a remarkably short life to be quickly snatched up by operators from all sectors — NBC, SBG, PTE, municipal and independent — and for use overseas.

The Fleetline's best sales years were in the 1970s when an average of over 650 a year entered service with British operators. London's big orders helped the totals but

Top:
Eastern Coach Works bodywork was built on Fleetline chassis for a number of operators, including Harper Bros of Heath Hayes, the Midlands independent. This 1973 CRL6 with 76-seat body was one of two new in 1973. They passed with the Harper business to Midland Red the following year. Roy Marshall

Above left:
Many other Fleetlines for independent operators were like this bus delivered to Blue Ensign of Doncaster in 1976, with a standard Roe 'independent' body. This 78-seat CRG6LX passed to South Yorkshire PTE with the Blue Ensign business in 1978. M. Fowler

Left:
SBG companies bought 640 Fleetlines between 1965 and 1980. Many had Alexander D-type 75-seat low-height bodywork, like this Alexanders (Midland) 1976 CRG6LXB in Perth. Stewart J. Brown

hindered deliveries to other fleets. The combination of the move of production to Leyland, the Gardner engine shortage, and the national industrial problems of 1973/74, meant that Fleetline deliveries suffered more than any others.

In 1976 some buses ordered for 1973 delivery was still awaited and the backlog in chassis availability had an inevitable knock-on effect with bodybuilders. The model never really quite recovered from these problems and the 1978 announcement that Fleetline production would cease within two years caused a further fall in demand as operators sought replacement models — not necessarily from Leyland.

Total Fleetline production amounted to 11,747 chassis, with 7,224 built at Coventry and the rest at Leyland; of these, 10,328 were home-market double-deckers.

Above right:
Scottish independents also bought Alexander-bodied Fleetlines, in this case a normal-height Alexander A-type 74-seater on FE30ALR chassis, one of two delivered in 1976 to AA Motor Services of Ayr. The choice of Leyland engines was unusual for Dodds, who owned the bus, and may have been a consequence of the Gardner engine supply problems. Malcolm Keeley

Right:
London Transport's last 400 Fleetlines were special quiet-pack buses with Leyland 690 engines, model FE30ALR Special, hence the unusual shapes around the engine compartment. This 1978 bus had Park Royal 71-seat two-door bodywork. R. L. Wilson

Below:
A long-wheelbase Fleetline with Northern Counties bodywork supplied to the Gloucestershire independent Cottrell of Mitcheldean, a 1978 FE33AGR with Northern Counties 83-seat bodywork. Malcolm Keeley

Left:
In 1980 Leon of Finningley bought this FE30AGR Fleetline with SBG-style 75-seat Alexander AD-type bodywork, complete with SBG destination layout. It was similar to buses supplied that same year to Alexanders (Midland) and Western SMT. S. J. Butler

Below:
The last Fleetline chassis built was a 1980 FE30ALR bodied by ECW and supplied in 1981 to South Notts. Note the Daimler badge on what was strictly a *Leyland* Fleetline.
Roger Kaye

Right:
Not a Fleetline, but a rear-engined Daimler double-decker all the same. The unique 1968 Daimler CRC6-36 with 86-seat two-door (front and rear) body by Northern Counties, supplied to Walsall Corporation. This 36ft bus with 18ft 6in wheelbase had a Cummins V6-200 engine mounted in the offside rear corner. It was to be the only CRC6-36 for a British operator, although 16 were supplied to the Johannesburg municipal fleet in South Africa. Malcolm Keeley

Below right:
A normal-length Fleetline chassis, showing the drop-centre rear axle which allowed a flat saloon floor and, in consequence, low-height bodies. Daimler

3 Rear-Engined Routemaster

Wheelbase: 5.13m (16ft 10in)
Engine: AEC AV691 11.3-litre naturally-aspirated six-cylinder diesel
Rating: 150bhp @ 1,800rpm
Gearbox: AEC fully-automatic electro-pneumatically controlled 4-speed epicyclic
Retarder: No
Brakes: Power hydraulic
Steering gear: AEC worm and nut with hydraulic power assistance
Rear axle: Spiral bevel, fully-floating
Suspension: Coil spring front (independent), air suspension rear (rigid axle)

The Model

Under normal circumstances AEC would probably have developed its own rear-engined double-deck chassis, following Leyland's and Daimler's lead. Its mainstream front-engined double-deck range was the well-established Regent family and its more recent models were still resolutely front-engined — the Bridgemaster (1956) and Renown (1962). It also produced the Routemaster for London Transport, and although this was available on the open market, only BEA (with LT connections anyway) and Northern General bought the model.

It seems likely that the merger with Leyland may have stifled AEC's ambitions, but pressure from London Transport produced the concept of a rear-engined Routemaster, a natural progression.

Work started on designing the bus in 1964 and five were to be built initially. London would receive one, three demonstrators would be built, and AEC would retain one for development work. It was rumoured that at least one in municipal colours would appear at the 1966 Commercial Motor Show and that Leeds and Sheffield Corporations, Northern General and Yorkshire Traction were all interested. As it turned out, no bus was displayed.

The first — and only — bus was completed late in 1966, a bus for London Transport that clearly owed much to the standard Routemaster and apparently used around 60% of RM parts.

The specification was very advanced in comparison with the Atlantean and Fleetline and included features which were not offered on another model until Leyland's Titan appeared a decade later.

The London bus, FRM1, entered service in June 1967 alongside LT Atlanteans, but in 1969 was moved to work in the Croydon area as a one-man operated bus. It later moved to Potters Bar and ended its active life on the Round London Sightseeing Tour. It was withdrawn from service in 1984 and retained for preservation by the London Transport Museum.

The promise of FRM1 was never realised, killed at an early stage by Leyland, who saw the Atlantean as its main double-deck model. Had AEC been able to persevere, the response to the rear-engined Routemaster might have been little different to the limited response to the later Leyland Titan. But if London Transport had stuck with the FRM, instead of getting disastrously involved in AEC Merlin and Swift single-deckers, and Daimler Fleetline double-deckers, the class might have grown to over 3,000 buses.

Below:
The bus that could have been the first of many, but stayed unique — the rear-engined Routemaster FRM1. The Routemaster ancestry is very obvious. It is seen in 1986 at the Clydeside Scottish open day at Greenock, believed to be its longest foray out of London. John Burnett

4 Bristol VRT

VRT/SL, VRT/LL
Wheelbase: 4.93m (16ft 2in) (VRT/LL: 5.64m [18ft 6in])
Engine: Gardner 6LXB 10.45-litre naturally aspirated six-cylinder diesel
Rating: 165bhp @ 1,700rpm
Gearbox: Bristol/SCG epicycylic semi-automatic
Retarder: No
Brakes: Dual air system
Steering gear: Burman recirculatory ball type
Rear axle: Double reduction drop centre
Suspension: Steel semi-elliptic type leaf springs
Options: Fully-automatic gearbox

VRT3/SL, VRT3/LH
Wheelbase: (4.93m) (16ft 2in) (VRT3/LH: 5.64m [18ft 6in])
Engine: Gardner 6LXB 10.45-litre naturally aspirated six-cylinder diesel
Rating: 188bhp @ 1,850rpm
Gearbox: SCG 5-speed semi-automatic direct air-operated epicyclic
Retarder: No
Brakes: Air-operated dual-line split system
Steering gear: Recirculating ball type with integral hydraulic power assistance
Rear axle: Bristol double-reduction drop-centre with differential between spiral and spur grears
Suspension: Semi-elliptic overslung leaf springs
Options: Leyland 510 8.2-litre turbocharged engine
Leyland G2 fully-automatic gearbox control system

The Model

Bristol Commercial Vehicles was in the unusual position of having a restricted yet monopoly market. Its roots were in the Bristol Tramways operating company and it was nationalised with the parent Tilling group in 1948 along with bodybuilders Eastern Coach Works. The Bristol/ECW combination then became the standard chassis/body combination for Tilling companies and was otherwise only available to fellow nationalised undertakings, principally London Transport and SBG; London did buy ECW bodies and SBG Bristol/ECW vehicles (as well as Bristol chassis with Alexander bodies), but they were also able to shop on the open market.

Tilling's principal double-deck model in the 1950s was the Bristol/ECW Lodekka, the archetypal low-height front-engined model, which was supplied at a rate of roundly 350-400 a year. The Lodekka had seats for up to 70 passengers, and 78 in extended form, but had enjoyed a long production life and was ready for replacement by the early 1960s.

The answer being offered was the Bristol VRL, a rear-engined chassis introduced in 1966, but with the Gardner 6LX engine mounted longtitudinally in the rear offside corner rather than transversely as on the Atlantean and Fleetline. It was a brave concept, but pressure from operators necessitated a more conventional approach. A further VR model, the VRT, appeared in 1968, with a transverse Gardner 6LX engine. It had a drop centre rear axle and therefore had the same flexibility as the Fleetline.

VRT output was initially much lower than the Lodekka had been, and until 1973 the model annually averaged little more than 10% of the double-deck market. The VRT was affected by some of the problems that delayed Fleetline production in the early 1970s, and one answer was the Series 3 VRT with Leyland's 510 engine and revised cooling arrangements and a totally encapsulated engine/gearbox unit, in an effort to reduce engine noise.

The revised VRT boosted sales and from 1976 output rose to record levels — 1980 being its best-ever year with 600 delivered.

In spite of this, production ceased in 1981 to make space for Leyland's Bristol-built Olympian.

The Market

The VRT started out as a Tilling group model and inevitably most of its early successes were in this sector, and with SBG companies which received some of the first production examples. SBG quickly tired of the VRT, but the Tilling companies and their NBC successors were the main customers. Some may have taken the VRT reluctantly, the former BET firms that had big Atlantean or Fleetline fleets, but some of the more obvious 'Leyland' customers like Northern General, Ribble and Southdown were able to buy Atlanteans in the 1970s because of VRT supply problems.

Surprisingly, several of the PTEs became good VRT customers. None of their constituents had any real Bristol experience in recent years, yet Merseyside and West Midlands bought batches in 1973-76, and SELNEC took 25 that had been ordered by the North Western company.

Municipal customers grew over the years, with fleets like Burnley & Pendle, Great Yarmouth, Lincoln and North-

Right:
Tyne & Wear PTE bought six of the Ribble group's 1972 Bristol VRL/LH6L coaches in 1976 for special services to the Tyne Commission Quay. They had ECW 60-seat bodies. Malcolm Keeley

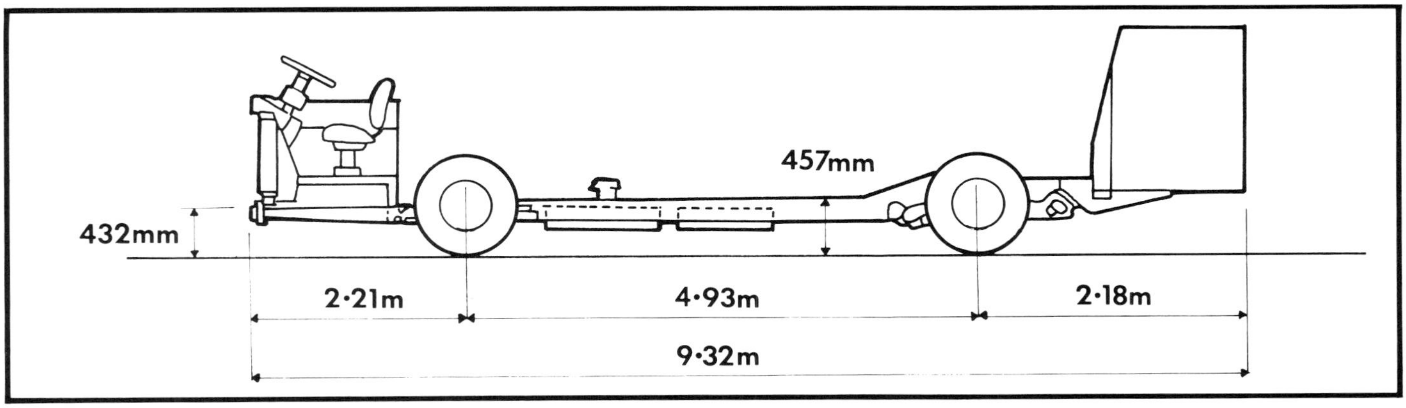

ampton taking respectable numbers. Even independents chose the VRT — from Hutchings & Cornelius in 1973 to Mayne, Manchester and Stevenson, Uttoxeter.

When VR production stopped in 1981, some 4,531 had been built, of which nearly 80% had been for NBC companies or their predecessors.

Left:
One of the two Bristol VRL/SL6X prototypes that were first shown at the 1966 Commercial Motor Show. This was the Central SMT example, that entered service in 1967, although it was still owned by Bristol. The longitudinal engine layout did not prove popular. Stewart J. Brown

Below:
Another SBG fleet, Scottish Omnibuses, received the first production Bristol VRTs. These were VRT/LL6G models, 33ft long, with ECW 83-seat bodies, new in 1968. These were the only 33ft VRTs bodied by ECW. It passed with SBG's other VRTs to NBC, and this bus ended up with Eastern Counties in 1973. The extra length is apparent. Malcolm Keeley

Above:
PTE fleets bought VRTs to boost their new vehicle intake. Merseyside PTE took 50 of these VRT/SL6G in 1974 with East Lancs 74-seat bodies. Roy Marshall

Right:
NBC operators who did not need low-height bodies received normal-height ECW-bodied VRTs like this 1977 London Country example. The broad white band emphasises the rather ungainly nature of the adaptation of a body style that was designed for much lower buses. This VRT/SL6L was one of 15 sold to Bristol Omnibus in 1980/81, as they were non-standard in the London Country Atlantean-dominated fleet. R. L. Wilson

Bottom right:
Independents also bought ECW-bodied VRTs, like this VRT/SL3 with Gardner 6LXB engine and 70-seat coach-seated bodywork for Mayne of Manchester. It was one of three buses delivered in 1978, which were followed by another two in 1980. Roy Marshall

Facing page, top:
Among the last Bristol double-deckers built were VRT/SL3 6LXBs with 74-seat ECW bodies for Eastern Counties, delivered in 1981. This bus passed with others to Cambus, the fleet formed to take over the western part of the Eastern Counties area. Mike Greenwood

Facing page, bottom:
One of the major features that marked the Bristol VRT as different from the Atlantean and Fleetline was the front-mounted radiator. This is a VRT/SL2 chassis with Gardner 6LXB engine. Bristol

47 SERVICE
SUITES
EASTERN COUNTIES
VR279
VAH 279X
CARPETS
SHOP AT
HOME
SERVIC

5 Leyland Atlantean AN68 series

AN68D/1R, AN68D/2R

Wheelbase: 4.95m (16ft 3in) (AN68D/2R: 5.64m [18ft 6in])
Engine: Leyland 680 11.1-litre naturally aspirated six-cylinder diesel
Rating: 174bhp @ 1,900rpm
Gearbox: Leyland 5-speed close-ratio Pneumocyclic, semi-automatic control
Retarder: No
Brakes: Dual-line full air, split system. Diaphragm operation
Steering gear: Cam and double roller type with power assistance
Rear axle: Leyland single-reduction with spiral bevel crown wheel
Suspension: Semi-elliptic springs
Options: Fully-automatic gearbox control

The Model

The revamped AN68 Atlantean chassis appeared not a moment too soon. The old PDR model was being easily outstripped in sales terms by Daimler's Fleetline, and a third rear-engined model, the Bristol VRT, was on the market. Although all these models were products of the same manufacturing giant, British Leyland, each had its followers and Leyland was anxious not to lose them. These three models had an absolute monopoly of the double-deck market, as all the front-engined chassis had been phased out by 1969, victims of Bus Grants, Leyland rationalisation and changing market requirements.

The main difference on the AN68 was that the 680 engine had become standard (it had been an option on the PDR since 1966), and close attention was paid to the engine cooling system. Power-assisted steering became standard on the longer AN68/2R, and optional on the more familiar AN68/1R.

Modifications to the Atlantean were marked by suffixes in the chassis designation. The AN68A had the rationalised G2 gearbox control system; the AN68B had F&M fuel pump, air throttle and fully-automatic gearbox with LVA45 control as standard; the AN68C reverted to the semi-automatic gearbox as standard; the AN68D had the rationalised 680 engine. Many of South Yorkshire PTE's later Atlanteans had (non-standard) Voith gearboxes.

The Atlantean was finally killed by new EEC regulations, but continued until 1986 as a successful export model. In its 27-year life nearly 12,000 Atlanteans were sold to British operators and some 57% of these were AN68 variants. The PTEs were the biggest market sector with considerable sales to municipalities, NBC fleets and their BET group predecessors, and even independents.

The Market

Leyland now had a new set of customers to supply. Many municipal Atlantean customers were now fused into the big PTEs — Merseyside, SELNEC, Tyneside and West Midlands. Of the 20 undertakings that were replaced in 1969/70 by PTEs, nine were good Atlantean customers, including major fleets like Bolton, Liverpool, Manchester and Newcastle. Any change of vehicle policy would have been disastrous for the Atlantean's future, particularly following the creation of the NBC. The former BET group fleets, including Atlantean stalwarts like Northern General and Ribble, were now in the hands of a group with a built-in bus manufacturing facility at Bristol and ECW; granted, Leyland had an interest in Bristol/ECW products, but it seemed obvious where NBC would buy its buses.

Above left:
Similar Northern Counties bodywork to that on the Cottrell Fleetline already illustrated was fitted to this 1972 Leyland Atlantean AN68/2R 82-seater for The Delaine, Bourne, although the livery application on Delaine buses has always been ornate. Roy Marshall

Left:
An Atlantean that remained unique was this 1976 South Yorkshire PTE AN68A/1R which received Van Hool McArdle 70-seat, two-door bodywork of a style previously supplied to the PTE on Volvo Ailsa chassis. Other VHMA-bodied Atlanteans were built for CIE in Ireland, but these had square-looking bodies. Stewart J. Brown

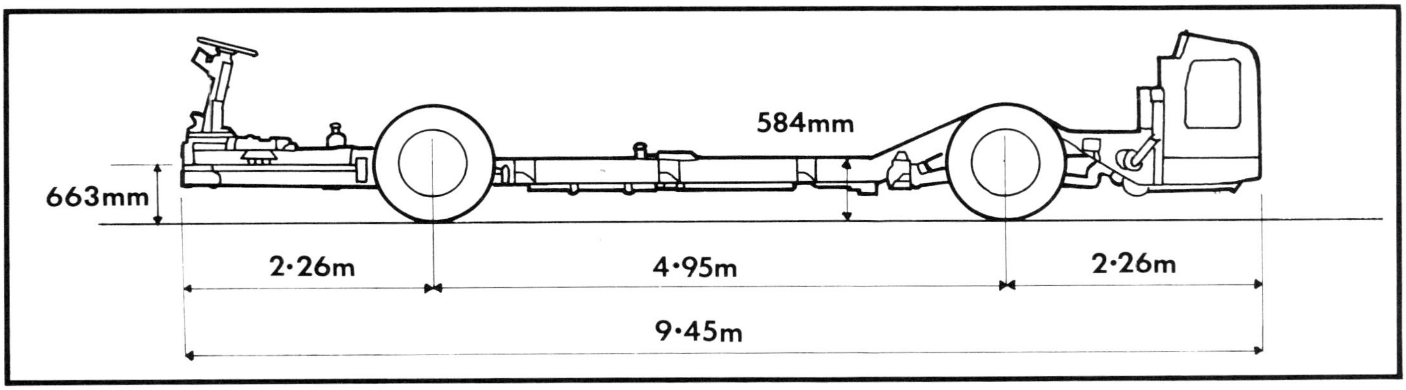

Fortunately for Leyland, three of the new PTEs came up with big Atlantean orders; the Merseyside, SELNEC and Tyneside undertakings became major Atlantean customers and for a period nine out of every 10 home-market Atlanteans was for a PTE or municipality. When more PTEs were created in 1973/74 they too

Above:
Tyne & Wear PTE bought Atlanteans for use in Newcastle, but Fleetlines were ordered for the Sunderland area. A PTE Atlantean AN68A/2R with Alexander 86-seat, two-door body, one of 70 bought in 1978, leads a Fleetline FE30AGR with MCW 75-seat, one-door body along the seafront at Seaburn.
S. J. Butler

Right:
Northern General was one of the NBC fleets able to buy Atlanteans in addition to Bristol VRTs. In Newcastle, painted in Northern's original concession to Tyne & Wear yellow, is a 1980 AN68B/1R with Roe 73-seat bodywork to a style that had previously been built by Park Royal. R. L. Wilson

chose Atlanteans — South and West Yorkshire, and Greater Glasgow replaced municipals that had been faithful customers. Not all PTEs were entirely faithful, though. Most bought other rear-engined double-deckers, sensibly keeping their options open; only West Midlands resisted the Atlantean's appeal.

NBC returned to Leyland for Atlanteans in 1976 because of delays in building Bristol VRTs, and until 1981 a small group of NBC fleets received Park Royal, Roe or ECW bodied examples — all built within the Leyland empire.

By 1979 even the AN68 was long in the tooth compared with the rash of new competing models, but it was market leader with an impressive 36%; its best production year was 1981, with 670 delivered to British operators, a very close second to the Metrobus with 677. This was to be the Atlantean's swansong. By now the replacement Olympian was being produced and although home market production continued until 1984, output and market share dropped. Even in its final year, though, it comfortably outsold the Ailsa, Citybus, Dominator and Scania.

Some big customers, like Merseyside and Greater Manchester, stuck with Atlanteans right to the end, building up substantial fleets over many years. One *new* customer in 1983 was Barrow which came along with an order for three followed by a fourth bus in 1984.

Top right:
Other NBC Atlanteans had ECW bodywork, like this 1981 Trent AN68C/1R with 74-seat body. Trent had been an early Atlantean user before switching to Fleetlines, but returned to the Atlantean later in its life. Roy Marshall

Above right:
Similar bodywork was built for an unusual Atlantean sold to Fishwick of Leyland in 1981. It was built on an AN69A/1R chassis, an experimental model with the turbocharged 690 engine, complete with rear end similar to London Transport's 400 B20 Fleetlines. M. Fowler

Right:
Kingston-upon-Hull Corporation bought many Atlanteans, and this 1982 AN68C/1R with one-door Roe 74-seat body was one of its last. Roy Marshall

Left:
An unexpected late customer for the Atlantean was Barrow Corporation, who in 1983 received three AN68D/1R with Greater-Manchester-style Northern Counties 75-seat bodies, and bought another in 1984. John Burnett

Below:
Fishwick of Leyland received another unique experimental Atlantean in 1984, an AN69/2R, again with the 690 engine, fitted with ECW bodywork of a style more normally associated with Olympians. The AN69 was mainly an export model for Iran. Leyland

Above and below:
Two of the bigger Atlantean customers stuck with the model right to the end, with only small batches of newer models to compensate. The 1984 Greater Manchester AN68D/1R, outside the refurbished frontage of Manchester's Victoria railway station, had Northern Counties light alloy standard 75-seat bodywork, as did most of the PTE's Atlanteans. The Merseyside bus was the PTE's last Atlantean, a 1984 AN68D/1R with Alexander 75-seat bodywork to a style that had been built for the undertaking for 13 years. It is seen on the test-track at Leyland during the Leyland Vehicles 90th anniversary weekend in 1986. R. L. Wilson

The Second Generation

6 Metro-Scania Metropolitan

BR111DH
Wheelbase: 5.13m (16ft 10in)
Engine: Scania D11 C06 11-litre six-cylinder diesel
Rating: 200bhp @ 2,200rpm
Gearbox: Scania fully-automatic
Retarder: No
Brakes: Air-operated twin circuit split system
Steering gear: ZF recirculating ball with independent hydraulic power assistance
Rear axle: Scania RA651 spiral bevel
Suspension: Full air with rolling lobe bellows

The Model

At the end of the 1960s the British bus industry was going through major changes. There was the creation of NBC, the formation of the first PTEs, the introduction of the Bus Grants system, and the emergence of British Leyland.

For the manufacturers outside British Leyland control, and there were very few of these, there was a danger that all of these events could have a disastrous effect. Metro-Cammell Weymann (MCW) had long relied on bodybuilding business from municipal and BET group customers and from London Transport. Now many of the best municipalities were disappearing into the PTEs; and the BET group had sold out to the Transport Holding Company to form the basis of NBC — complete with its close connections with Leyland.

One way of protecting its interests was for MCW to become involved more deeply in manufacturing. For 20 years, MCW had worked sporadically with Leyland in the development of integral buses, but Leyland's expansion had rendered this type of liaison unlikely in the future. MCW therefore sought partners elsewhere and in 1969 announced a joint venture with the Swedish builder Scania — an integral single-deck city bus, the Metro-Scania.

Below:
The Metro-Scania Metropolitan introduced a new shape on Britain's urban streets. The asymmetrical lower-deck windscreen was a ready identification feature carried over from the earlier Metro-Scania single-deck model. The engine was not isolated in a separate compartment, and later models from other builders echoed this arrangement. Greater Manchester PTE bought 10 of these BR112DH models in 1974, with 73-seat bodies, and one is seen in Bury in 1978 on the Trans-Lancs Express service. Malcolm Keeley

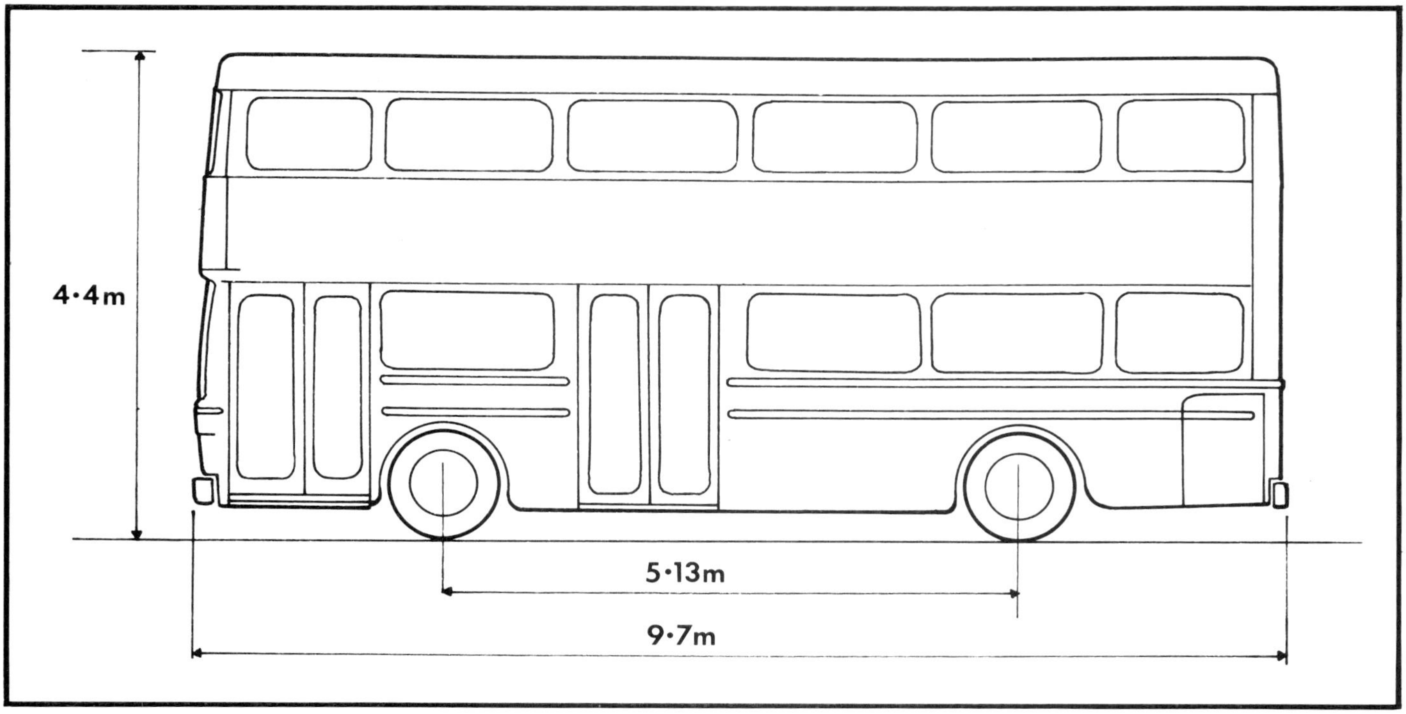

This advanced specification bus was based on the Scania BR111MH underframe with bodywork built by MCW in Birmingham, and it sold in respectable numbers in 1970-73.

The next logical stage was a double-deck equivalent and this materialised as the Metropolitan late in 1973. Based on the Scania BR111DH, it was an integral 9.7m (31ft 10in) bus with seats for up to 76 passengers. The Scania engine was mounted transversely at the rear and full air suspension was featured — the first British double-decker so fitted.

The Metropolitan's life on the British market was brief — it was in production for only five years — but its successes were impressive, particularly as it was introducing new mechanical units to Britain in the face of Leyland's monopoly. Its contemporary, the front-engined Ailsa, was less immediately successful and though it outsold the Metropolitan overall, this was achieved over a 10-year period.

Although the Metropolitan's life was brief, its progeny were the MCW Metrobus and the Scania BR112DH, which followed in 1978/80.

Above right:
The Metropolitan was a highly-standardised model, and only liveries changed its appearance. Newport Corporation bought 10 in 1975 with 73-seat bodies, and became a firm Scania fan. R. L. Wilson

Right:
NBC ordered five Metropolitans for evaluation and allocated them to Maidstone & District. New in 1975, they had 75-seat bodies. S. J. Butler

The Market

For many fleets, the Metropolitan represented a protest vote. There was dissatisfaction with the Atlantean/Fleetline/VRT monopoly and Leyland's apparent inflexibility. Here was an advanced-specification vehicle with sparkling performance that could be bought in a highly-standardised form from a single supplier — no hassle with separate chassis and body sourcing.

In its first year in full production, 1975, more than 200 were sold, capturing over 10% of the double-deck market. Most of these were sales to frustrated PTEs, but they also included substantial municipal deliveries to Hull (20) and Leicester (35).

London Transport bought 164 in 1976/77, while over the same period Tyne & Wear PTE became the second biggest customer with 144.

The last deliveries were early in 1978, to Hull and Reading. In just five years, 659 had been delivered to British customers.

Above left:
Tyne & Wear PTE bought 140 Metropolitans between 1975 and 1977. This was one of 50 new in 1976, some with one-door bodies and others, as here, with separate entrances and exits. R. L. Wilson

Left:
Leicester City Transport had also bought the single-deck Metro-Scania, and bought 68 of the double-deck Metropolitan. A 1976 example with 75-seat body. Roy Marshall

Below:
Kingston-upon-Hull progressed from Metropolitans to its all-MCW successor, the Metrobus. A 1975 Metropolitan is seen (right) alongside a 1980 Metrobus. The broad similarity is evident, although the asymmetric widscreen was less pronounced on the Metrobus. M. Fowler

This picture:
London Transport's nippy Metropolitans seemed to suffer a disproportionate amount of accident damage. These three sad-looking buses were among six lying at Kingston in 1979. Ian Cowley

Below:
Reading bought new Metropolitans and in 1983 bought 21 of the ex-London Transport vehicles that were available on the market. Two of the London buses are seen in Broad Street, Reading, in 1984. S. J. Butler

7 Foden-NC

Wheelbase: 5.11m (16ft 9in)
Engine: Gardner 6LXB 10.45-litre naturally-aspirated six-cylinder diesel
Rating: 172bhp @ 1,750rpm
Gearbox: Allison MT640 fully-automatic 4-speed
Retarder: Ferodo
Brakes: Air-operated twin-circuit split system
Steering gear: Burman fully-integral power
Rear axle: Newage double-reduction drop-centre
Suspension: Semi-elliptic leaf springs

Left:
Greater Manchester PTE was the only Foden-NC customer to take more than one example. This was the first of two, new in 1976, and both had Northern Counties 75-seat bodies. The body is clearly based on the Manchester standard, but longer, and with the Foden-NC badge on the front panel.
P. Sykes

Below:
The West Midlands PTE Foden-NC was delivered in 1978, with 76-seat Northern Counties body, but was withdrawn from service prematurely. Malcolm Keeley

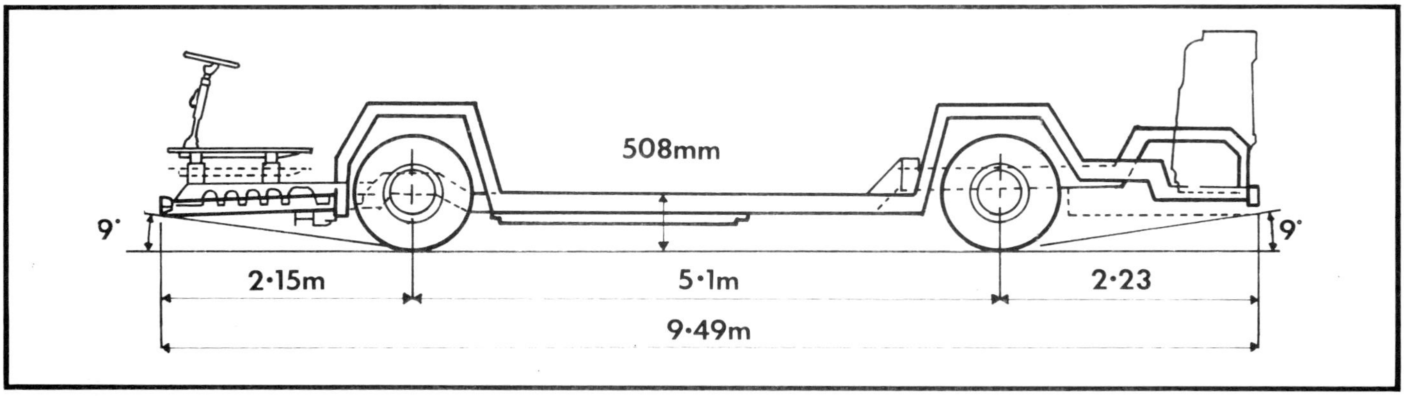

The Model

The name Foden has always been closely associated with heavy trucks, yet in the prewar period, and more particularly in the years after World War 2, the company tried hard to enter the bus and coach market.

The last front-engined Foden double-deckers were delivered in 1956, and the company concentrated on trucks. But with the renewed interest in the double-deck

Right:
Derby was the only municipal customer for the Foden-NC; a 73-seat bus was delivered in 1978. Roy Marshall

Below:
NBC allocated its Foden-NC to Potteries, a low-height bus (like the West Yorkshire PTE example), with 74-seat body new in 1978. The poster on the side refers to the evaluation tests involving the Foden, but the message can have made little sense to the average passer-by. Roy Marshall

bus market and the imminent demise of the Daimler Fleetline, Foden decided to re-enter the fray.

In 1976 Foden and bodybuilders Northern Counties unveiled the Foden-NC, a double-deck model with a drop-centre rear axle (and therefore a low-height capability), and a rear-mounted Gardner 6LXB engine and Allison automatic gearbox.

The involvement of Northern Counties was interesting. This well-established Wigan-based coachbuilder had a small and faithful band of customers and a good reputation for the quality of its products. But it had no doubt observed how other bodybuilders were becoming more closely linked with chassis manufacturers — Alexander's involvement in the development of the Ailsa, MCW with Scania — and would be conscious of Leyland's declared intent to develop an integral double-deck model, which could have had as serious an effect on bodybuilders as the success of the Leyland National single-deck city bus.

Only seven of the Foden-NC model were actually completed — six with Northern Counties bodies, the seventh with an East Lancs body — before it was decided once again to concentrate on truck production.

The Market

When only seven examples of a double-deck model are built, it is possible to detail each one. Four were normal-height buses: two for Greater Manchester PTE, one for West Midlands PTE and one for Derby City Transport. Two were low-height: for Potteries and West Yorkshire PTE, and one was a normal-height bus with East Lancs body for South Yorkshire PTE.

All were withdrawn prematurely.

Above:
The only Foden-NC that did not receive Northern Counties bodywork was the South Yorkshire PTE example which had an East Lancs 74-seat two-door body. Roy Marshall

Below:
The Foden-NC underframe was an early example of the perimeter-frame construction that allows bodybuilders to integrate the body structure to the underframe. Foden

8 Dennis Dominator

Wheelbase: 4.95m (16ft 3in) (long wheelbase: 5.64m [18ft 6in])
Engine: Gardner 6LXB 10.45-litre naturally-aspirated six-cylinder diesel
Rating: 185bhp @ 1,850rpm
Gearbox: Voith D851 3-speed fully-automatic
Retarder: Integral
Brakes: Full air horizontal split system
Steering gear: Hydraulic power-assisted
Rear axle: Dennis drop-centre double-reduction (low-height); GKN straight beam hub reduction axle (normal height)
Suspension: Semi-elliptic leaf springs
Options: Rolls-Royce Eagle 220 Mk III engine, developing 180bhp @ 1,850rpm
DAF DK1160V engine, developing 180bhp @ 1,850rpm
Voith D854 4-speed fully-automatic gearboxes
Maxwell 4-speed fully-automatic gearboxes
Full air self-levelling suspension

The Model

Dennis had been one of the earliest British bus builders although it had never been a volume producer like AEC or Leyland.

In the 1950s it had obtained the rights to build the Bristol Lodekka under licence for non-nationalised fleets, but in spite of the apparent appeal of such a model, the Dennis Loline was not a notable success, selling just under 300 to British operators between 1957 and 1967.

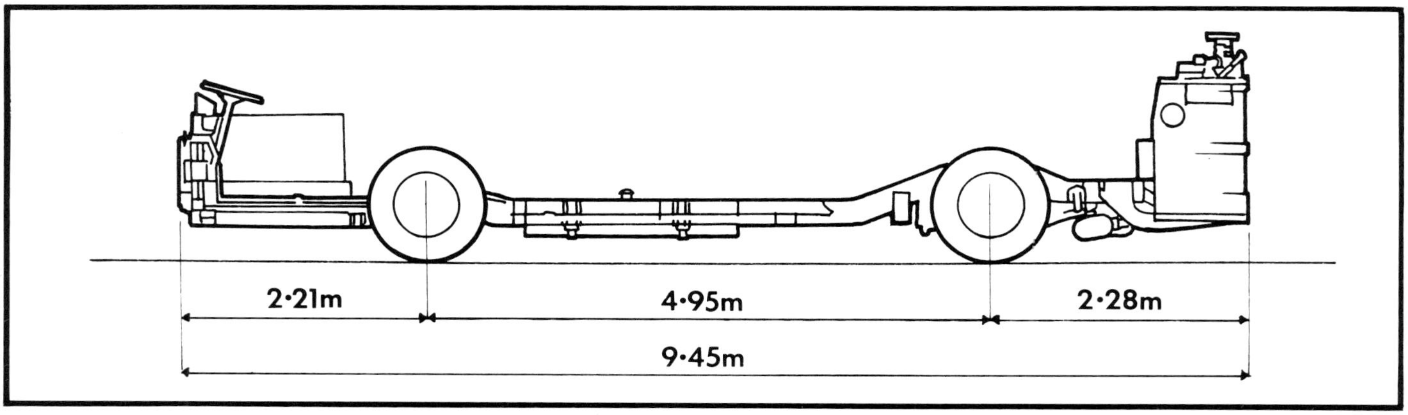

Bottom:
Potteries received NBC's first Dennis Dominator, a 1978 DD102 model with Alexander 74-seat body. It passed to join other Dominators at Maidstone & District in 1983. M. Fowler

With the forthcoming demise of the Daimler Fleetline, Dennis saw a market opportunity for a low-height Gardner-engined bus; Foden also saw this gap but failed to fill it. Dennis has been more successful.

In 1977 Dennis announced the Dominator, with transverse Gardner 6LXB engine and Voith gearbox. Initially it featured a drop-centre rear axle as standard, permitting low-height bodywork, but later a straight-axle version was offered.

Options offered were a longer-wheelbase version, the Rolls-Royce Eagle 220 engine, and the Maxwell automatic gearbox. Full air suspension was an option to leaf springs from 1980.

The Market

The Dominator has sold mainly to municipal and PTE customers and although seen as a Fleetline substitute, many of the buyers have been former Atlantean customers (like Blackburn, Brighton, Eastbourne, Hull, Hyndburn, Ipswich and Warrington).

The biggest single user has been South Yorkshire PTE which between 1978 and 1986 took nearly 400, the majority with Rolls-Royce engines. Other PTE customers have been Greater Manchester and Merseyside.

Company fleets choosing Dominators have been SBG fleets Central and Western, and in NBC only Maidstone & District and Potteries. A few independents have bought Dominators — AA, A1 and OK.

Dominator sales levels have been modest and without the South Yorkshire and export business might have been dangerously so. In its best year, 1982, the Dominator held 12% of the market for new double-deckers.

Top right:
East Staffordshire District Council bought three of these DD110A models in 1979, with a style of East Lancs body that is familiar on many Dominators. The East Staffordshire undertaking was merged with local independent Stevenson of Uttoxeter in 1985. Roy Marshall

Above right:
Long-wheelbase Dominators have been very rare. Bishop Auckland independent OK bought this 85-seat Northern Counties-bodied DD126A in 1980. Malcolm Keeley

Right:
Maidstone & District received six DD129 in 1980 with Willowbrook 74-seat bodies, for evaluation purposes. They have since been joined by second-hand Dominators from various sources. S. J. Butler

Right:
Leicester City Transport was involved in the early development of the Dominator, and has built up a sizeable fleet. This 1980 DD120 was one of five with unusual Marshall bodies.
R. L. Wilson

Below:
The biggest Dominator customer has been South Yorkshire PTE, with nearly 400 in the fleet. The most familiar type has Alexander R-type 78-seat bodywork similar to this 1982 DDA133 model. Mike Greenwood

Right:
Tayside Regional Transport bought five long-wheelbase DDA139 Dominators in 1982, fitted with two-door East Lancs 79-seat bodies, but sold them, along with an earlier short-wheelbase bus, in 1985. Roy Marshall

Above left:
Central Scottish was the first SBG fleet to choose Dominators, and this 1982 DD137B example has Alexander RL-type body. In SBG's 1985 restructuring this bus passed to the new Kelvin Scottish company.
Stewart J. Brown

Left:
Some Dominators have been sold by their original owners after a fairly short time, like this Central Scottish DD135B model with Alexander 76-seat body, new in 1981, and transferred with three others to Eastern Scottish in 1986. They were suitably painted and briefly operated before further transfer that same year to Clydeside Scottish.
John Burnett

Below:
Dennis did win over some former Fleetline customers, like Chester. On the left is a 1981 Dominator DD121B, and on the right a 1978 Leyland Fleetline FE30AGR; both have Northern Counties 72-seat bodies. Chester switched to Olympians for its 1985 order.
Malcolm Keeley

Left:
London's three Dominators were bought for testing alongside other new models in 1984. London H3, with Northern Counties 70-seat two-door body, passes a more traditional London bus at Roehampton, a 1966 Routemaster RML. S. J. Butler

Below:
Ipswich bought a Dennis Dominator and a Leyland Olympian, each with East Lancs bodies, for evaluation prior to replacing its Atlanteans. The Dominator is seen on a summer Sunday service at Shotley in 1985. Ian Cowley

Left:
A significant Dominator was the chassis used as the base for the experimental DTA1401 trolleybus built in 1984 for South Yorkshire PTE, which received an Alexander 80-seat R-type body. John Burnett

The Third Generation

9 Leyland Titan

TNLXB2RRSp
Wheelbase: 5.03m (16ft 6in)
Engine: Gardner 6LXB 10.45-litre naturally-aspirated six-cylinder diesel
Rating: 177bhp @ 1,850rpm
Gearbox: Hydracyclic 5-speed close-ratio, fully-automatic control
Retarder: Integral hydraulically-operated friction
Brakes: Power hydraulic — split system
Steering gear: Rack-and-pinion, power assisted
Rear axle: Double-reduction drop centre
Suspension: Front: independent, by a combination of torsion bars and self-levelling air suspension. Rear: self-levelling air suspension.
Options: Leyland TL11 engine (11.1-litre, developing 170bhp @ 1,850rpm) on TNTL11
Semi-automatic transmission
Leyland 5-speed wide-ratio Hydracyclic gearbox

The Model
Leyland's success with the integral National city bus led its designers to consider a similar approach to the double-deck question. Its double-deck range in the 1970s was ageing — Atlantean, Fleetline and VRT were all beginning to betray their earlier development compared with newer models like the Metropolitan, and an all-purpose replacement was conceived.

Project B15 was an integral normal-height double-decker which would be produced to a highly standardised specification. This included many advanced features — independent front suspension, power-hydraulic braking, automatic gearbox with retarder, power-assisted steering; many of these had appeared on London's legendary Routemaster but were not all available on contemporary chassis. A prototype was built in 1974 and entered service with London Transport, a prime target, in 1976. This bus had a turbocharged Leyland 510 engine, an unusual choice, but this engine was only used in the prototypes.

For some time there was doubt about whether the B15 would ever get past the concept stage, but in 1977 it was announced that it would go into full production as the Titan, built at the Park Royal coachworks in London. Labour problems led to new doubts about the Titan's future, but a transfer of production to the Leyland National factory at Workington guaranteed its continuity.

Production Titans had the Gardner 6LXB engine, the first Leyland with a non-Leyland power unit, although six London and five Manchester buses had Leyland's TL11 engine; and six other London buses had the naturally-aspirated L11.

By far the largest Titan customer was London Transport and when London orders ceased in 1984, so did Titan production. The grand total was 1,163 for British operators, and one for export to Hong Kong.

Below:
Three of the prototype Leyland B15s were sold to Leyland's local independent, Fishwick, and two of them, FHG 592S (Titan 02 of 1974) and BCK 706R (05 of 1977) with Park Royal bodies are seen in 1986. They were bought from Leyland in 1982. R. L. Wilson

The Market

London was an important potential market for the Titan and so B15 prototypes were sent to London Transport for evaluation. The bigger PTEs also showed an interest, and West Midlands received five early examples and Greater Manchester 15. Reading was the only municipal customer with batches in 1979 and 1983.

Other orders had been placed by PTEs (Greater Glasgow, Merseyside, South Yorkshire, West Yorkshire), municipalities (Cardiff, Lothian, Southend, Tayside), NBC (Maidstone & District) and SBG (Alexander Fife), but these were cancelled when the model's future became uncertain in the late 1970s.

Titan's main success was with London Transport, with 1,125 delivered between 1978 and 1984, and during this period it shared the LT market with MCW's Metrobus. Although Titan production was normally slower, in some years LT chose to concentrate on Titans and in others it dual-sourced. Titan's best year was 1982 when the bus was built at Workington at a rate of more than one per working day.

Above left:
Titan BCK 706R spent some time with Merseyside PTE, and was painted in full MPTE livery. It is seen in 1981 at West Kirby.
R. L. Wilson

Left:
West Midlands PTE bought five early Titans in 1978/79, TNLXB models with Park Royal 73-seat, one-door bodies, but these were later sold to London Transport. Malcolm Keeley

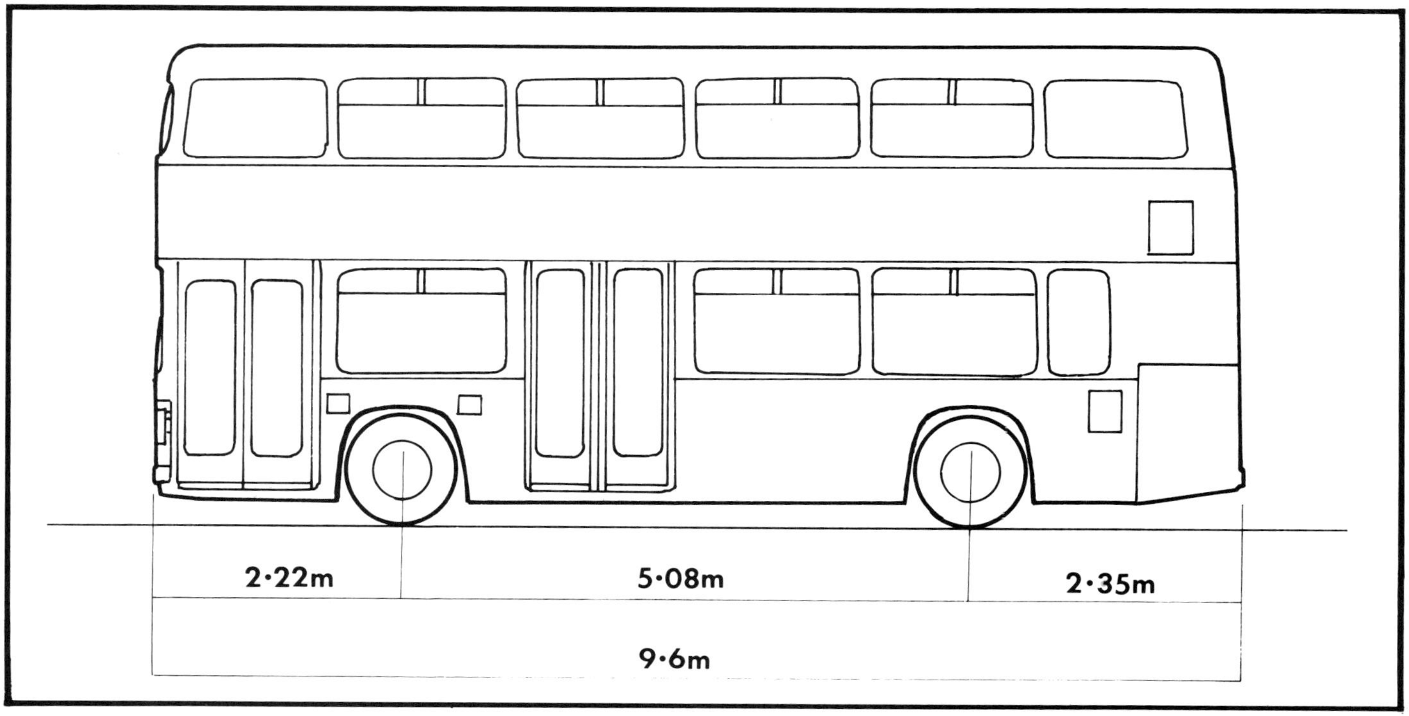

Above:
Titans of two of the biggest customers at Aldgate in 1983. The London bus on the left, one of 1,125, was a 1981 TNLXB2RRSp model with Workington-built Leyland 68-seat two-door body; the Reading bus, one of 12, was a 1982 TNLXCT with Leyland 66-seat one-door body, with coach seats for the Aldgate-Reading express service. Roy Marshall

Right:
Two of London's Titans were painted in this brighter livery for the express 177 service to Thamesmead in 1984, but otherwise the bus is a standard 1980 Park Royal-bodied example. Roy Marshall

Below:
The family resemblance between the Titan and its successor, the Olympian, is evident in this view at Bexleyheath in 1986. On the left is a new Olympian/ECW of London Buses, and on the right a 1983 Leyland-bodied Titan from the same fleet. S. J. Butler

10 MCW Metrobus

95 MDR

Wheelbase: 4.95m (16ft 3in)
Engine: Gardner 6LXB 10.45-litre naturally-aspirated six-cylinder diesel
Rating: 188bhp @ 1,850rpm
Gearbox: Voith D851 3-speed fully-automatic
Retarder: Three-stage integral
Brakes: Full air-operated dual-line split system
Steering gear: Integral power-assisted
Rear axle: Heavy-duty semi-drop hub reduction type
Suspension: Full air system
Options: Cummins L10 engine, developing 180bhp @ 1,850rpm
Rolls-Royce Eagle engine, developing 180bhp @ 1,850rpm
Hydraulic power-operated dual-line braking system
Voith D854 4-speed automatic transmission
Maxwell automatic gearbox

The Model
MCW's logical move after the brief success of the Metropolitan was to develop a complete integral double-deck model of its own. In 1977 this emerged as the Metrobus which featured the Gardner 6LXB engine, Voith gearbox and air suspension. Like Leyland's Titan it was aimed at the big urban fleets and quickly became familiar in Britain's main cities.

In 1979 three underframes with low-height Alexander bodies were supplied to Alexander (Midland), and several SBG, municipal and PTE customers have since chosen to take bodies on Metrobus by their normal suppliers.

The majority of Metrobuses have been supplied complete by MCW and in 1982 the original model was superseded by a simpler model, the Metrobus Mk II. London Transport chose to continue with the Mk I model, but other customers took the Mk II.

MCW developed its own low-height (4.19m, 13ft 9in) Metrobus in 1986 to satisfy NBC orders.

Left:
London Transport chose the MCW Metrobus to dual-source with the Leyland Titan. Both were high-specification integral vehicles with Gardner 6LXB engines, and this was M57, a 1979 DR101/9 example, in 1984 in a special London General livery. Stewart J. Brown

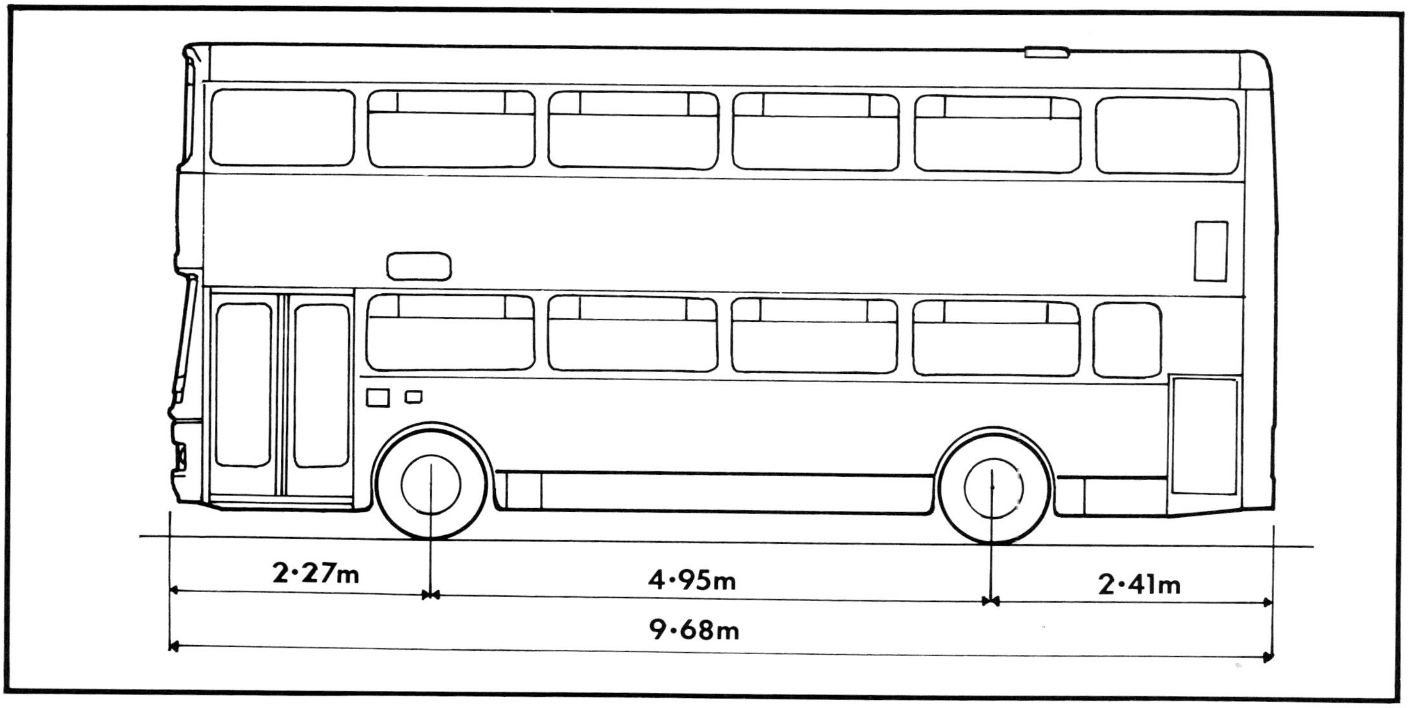

The Market

London Transport and West Midlands PTE have been easily the biggest Metrobus customers. London bought 1,440 Mk I and two experimental Mk II between 1978 and 1985, while West Midlands has taken nearly 1,000, changing to the Mk II in 1982.

The other PTEs have all bought Metrobuses in varying quantities, from Tyne & Wear's five to Greater Manchester's 200-plus. Municipal customers have been fewer — Hull, Leicester, Newport, Reading and Tayside. Some of the PTE and municipal Metrobuses have had other bodies, by Alexander and Northern Counties.

More surprising were the sales to NBC fleets, at first small batches to Bristol Omnibus, Maidstone & District and Northern General, but since joined by further deliveries to Northern General, and low-height buses for Yorkshire Traction.

The loss of the London business was a blow for MCW as more than 40% of the output was for LT in the 1980-84 period.

Above right:
With its requirement for lower-height buses, SBG turned to Alexander to body the Metrobus underframe. This was the Group's first, a 1979 DR102/3 with Alexander 73-seat body. Note the 'Metrobus' lettering on the grille. This body style was replaced by the neater RL type. Malcolm Keeley

Right:
Leicester bought four of these DR102/14 Metrobuses with two-door 72-seat bodies in 1980. Roy Marshall

Below:
Leicester also needed lower-height Metrobuses, and in 1983 received five DR102/35 with Alexander RL bodywork, seating 78, similar to SBG vehicles. Roy Marshall

The Metrobus has been the most successful of the third generation of rear-engined double-deckers, with home sales topping 3,000 in 1985. It outsold all other double-deck models in 1981, but Leyland's Olympian ran it a close second in 1982 and from then the two models ran virtually neck-and-neck.

Left:
Normal-height Alexander bodywork was built on Metrobus underframe for West Yorkshire PTE, as here, for Merseyside and Strathclyde PTEs. This DR101/15 of 1982 was one of 10.
Malcolm Keeley

Below:
After its Metropolitan experience, Newport ordered nine Metrobuses in the period when no Scania-engined bus was available on the market. This 1981 bus was type DR101/15, with 77-seat MCW body. M. Fowler

Right:
Bristol Omnibus chose five Metrobus DR103/4 in 1980, and when seen in 1984 this bus was lettered for the Bath fleet. It subsequently became part of the Badgerline fleet.
S. J. Butler

Left:
London's last two Metrobuses, numerically, were ordered as Mk II buses, being London's only examples of the standard provincial Metrobus. DR102/45 models, they entered service in 1984. A third bus was to join them, in effect a prototype of the Mk III Metrobus, but this was cancelled. Roy Marshall

Below:
The differences between the Mk I and Mk II Metrobuses are almost as subtle as between the Metropolitan and Metrobus. The Mk II bus on the left has a more normal windscreen, with straight lower edge, a slight lip to the upper front dome, and different glazing, which tends to emphasise the side pillar width. On the left, a South Yorkshire Transport 1986 DR102/53 model with Gardner 6LXCT engine and 70 coach seats for Fastline service, one of 10; on the right a 1980 DR102/13 with 73-seat two-door body, one of 50. S. J. Butler

The first Metrobuses to be bodied by Northern Counties were 10 with Cummins engines built in 1986 for GM Buses. These had 72-seat bodies with coach seats for express service.
Roy Marshall

Above:
Several operators have chosen the Mk II Metrobus for urban and interurban express work. Northern General bought 11 of these 72-seat vehicles for Expresslink work in 1986. Roy Marshall

This picture:
West Midlands Travel added coach-seated vehicles to its large Metrobus fleet in 1986 for Timesaver services. This 66-seat coach is passing a standard bus version.
Mike Greenwood

11 Scania N112DH

Wheelbase: 4.95m (16ft 3in) (long wheelbase: 5.64m [18ft 6in])
Engine: Scania DN11 11-litre naturally-aspirated six-cylinder diesel
Rating: 203bhp @ 2,220rpm
Gearbox: Scania GAV772R fully-automatic, 2-speed
Retarder: Integral hydraulic
Brakes: Dual-circuit direct-acting air
Steering gear: ZF integral power
Rear axle: Scania RV654 single-reduction spiral bevel
Suspension: Air
Options: Scania DS11 turbocharged engine, developing 253bhp @ 2,200rpm

The Model

Scania's involvement with MCW in the development of the Metro-Scania and Metropolitan models doubtless alerted the Swedish builders to the market potential for a wider range of options. In 1979 it was announced that Scania was 'coming back' and in 1980 the company showed the new BR112DH model, a variant of its 112 range, with 11-litre Scania engine, Voith automatic gearbox and air suspension. The model was redesignated N112DH and has also been built in single-deck form. Another double-deck model, the K92CR, with the 8.5-litre Scania DS9 engine, was ordered in 1986 by Maidstone Borough.

The Market

The Scania company's decision to enter a market that was already over populated was a brave and optimistic one. In the event, sales have been modest — less than 40 underframes in the first five years on the British market, and most of these to one customer, Newport, which had previously bought Metro-Scanias. Otherwise small batches of Scanias have gone to Leicester, Nottingham and Greater Manchester and Tyne & Wear PTEs, and a single vehicle to independent A1 Service.

Top left:
Nottingham received one of the earliest Scania BR112DH chassis, built in 1980 and fitted with East Lancs 78-seat bodywork. The air intake grille ahead of the offside rear wheel permits recognition of the few Scanias in service in Britain. Stewart J. Brown

Above left:
After its success with Metropolitans, Tyne & Wear PTE tried two Scania BR112DH with Alexander R-type 78-seat bodywork in 1982. The PTE's next large order was for similarly-bodied Leyland Olympians. S. J. Butler

Left:
Newport has been Scania's best double-deck customer; this Marshall-bodied 76-seat example was one of nine delivered in 1983. Newport has also used the N112DH chassis for single-deck buses. Roy Marshall

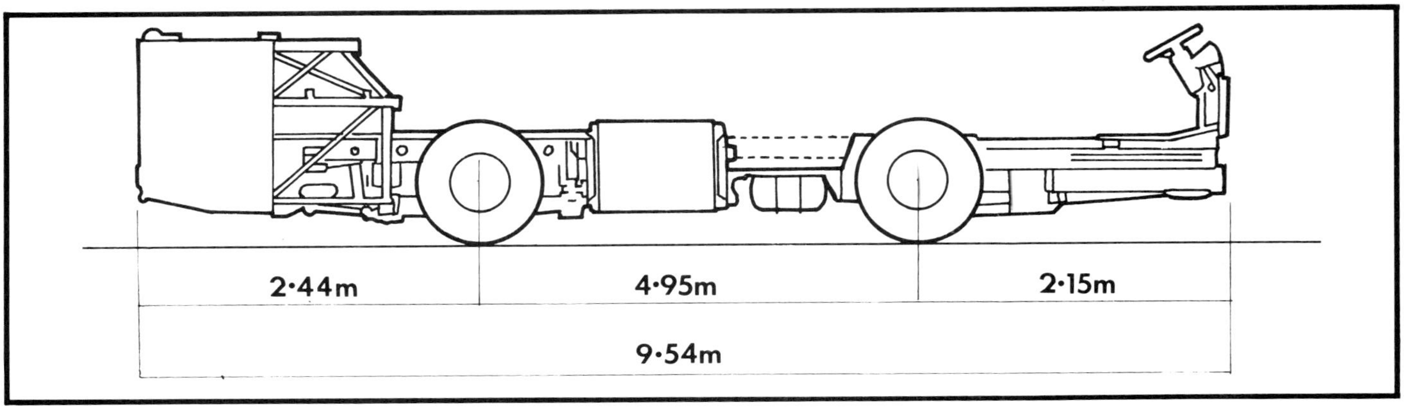

Right:
Leicester bought four of these N112DH Scanias in 1986 with East Lancs 79-seat bodies, and one is seen passing a Scania-engined Metropolitan. John Burnett

Below:
The Scania N112DH was largely similar to the British models with which it was introduced to compete, except for the radiator position, ahead of the offside rear axle rather than at the front end. Scania

12 Leyland Olympian

ONLXB/1R

Wheelbase: 4.95m (16ft 3in)
Engine: Gardner 6LXB 10.45-litre naturally-aspirated six-cylinder diesel
Rating: 177bhp @ 1,850rpm
Gearbox: Leyland 5-speed close-ratio Hydracyclic, semi-automatic control
Retarder: Integral hydraulically-operated friction
Brakes: Dual line full air, split system
Steering gear: Integral ZF power box
Rear axle: Leyland fully-floating double-reduction drop-centre with spiral bevel
Suspension: Full air
Options: Leyland TL11 engine, developing 170bhp @ 1,850rpm (ONTL11/1R)
Cummins L10 engine, developing 180bhp @ 1,850rpm (ONCL10/1R)
Leyland 5-speed wide-ratio Hydracyclic gearbox
Leyland fully-automatic gearbox control system
Voith D851 3-speed fully-automatic gearbox
Long wheelbase (ONLXB/2R and ONTL11/2R models: 5.64m [18ft 6in])

Above right:
Leyland Olympians of different operators, from different sectors, with different bodywork and different engine types, at Pontefract. On the left is an ONTL11/1R with Northern Counties 71-seat body, one of two delivered in 1982 to independent South Yorkshire Road Transport. On the right is a 1982 ONLXB/1R with ECW low-height 77-seat body from the nationalised West Riding fleet. M. Fowler

Right:
Lothian Region Transport has been the major operator of the longer-wheelbase ONTL11/2R model, with ECW two-door bodywork; they followed a large fleet of normal-length Alexander-bodied Atlanteans. The extra length of the body can be seen in the small extra window halfway along the body side, reminiscent of that on London's RML Routemasters. R. L. Wilson

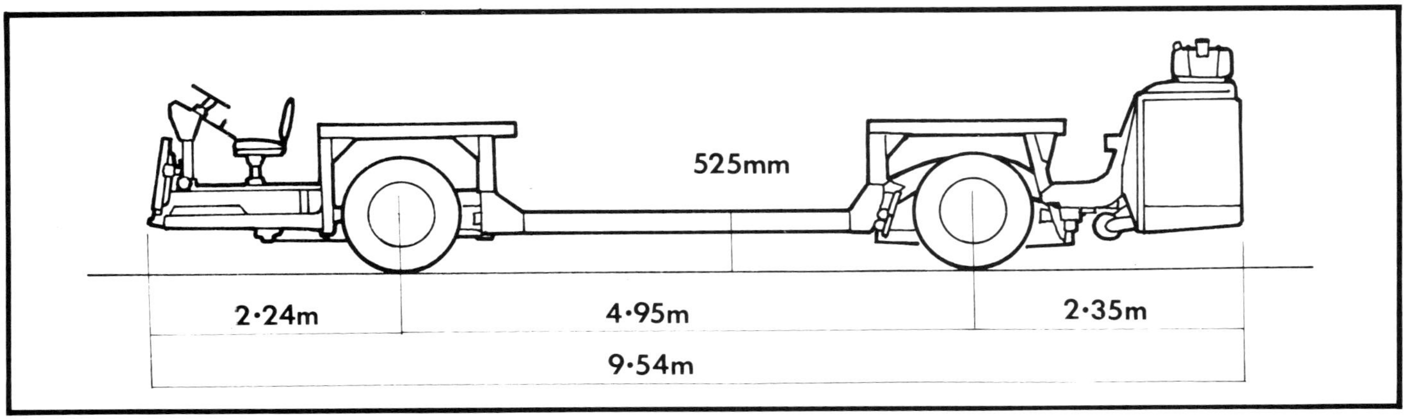

The Model

After the problems with operator resistance to the advanced specification of the integral Titan model, Leyland designed its double-deck model for the 1980s, coded B45, as a separate underframe incorporating the features expected, but not frighteningly over sophisticated.

The first Olympians were introduced in 1980 and following the lead of the Titan offered Gardner 6LXB or Leyland T11 engines. In practice the Gardner has been the more popular choice. It was also available in two wheelbase lengths, for 9.6m (31ft 6in) or 10.2m (33ft 5in) vehicles, and Leyland's Hydracyclic gearbox was standard.

Operator preference has produced Olympians with non-standard features like Voith gearboxes and Cummins engines.

The Olympian has a drop-centre rear axle, allowing low-height bodywork, for it was essentially replacing both the Bristol VRT and Leyland Atlantean.

Initially the underframe was built at Bristol but in 1983 production transferred to Workington after 995 had been delivered.

The Market

Although the formal links between NBC and Leyland had been broken in 1982 the Bristol VRT had been the principal NBC

Above:
Although South Yorkshire PTE has been buying large quantities of Dennis Dominators and MCW Metrobuses, it bought two Olympians in 1982. They were ONLXB/1R with Roe 76-seat bodies, and were built to West Yorkshire PTE standard. M. Fowler

Below:
Several NBC fleets have specified Olympians with coach-seated bodies, and Midland Red North took three of these ONLXB/1R with ECW 70-seat bodies in 1984. This one is seen in Midland Express livery at Tamworth.
R. L. Wilson

double-deck model until 1980 and it seemed likely that the Olympian would assume this mantle. VRT deliveries to NBC were still fairly high in 1981, the year production ceased, and only 60 Olympians entered service with the group as production built up.

In 1982 the entire double-deck order was Olympian, but while in 1983 over half Olympian production was for NBC fleets, the Metrobus squeezed in at Northern General and was to prove attractive to certain NBC companies.

The PTEs were initially slow to change to the Olympian, some having built up huge Atlantean fleets, and as late as 1983 more Atlanteans than Olympians were entering PTE service. With the run-down of home Atlantean production, the PTEs had less choice, but PTE deliveries have been fairly modest. Only Greater Manchester, Tyne & Wear and West Yorkshire have adopted the Olympian as a standard model, while Merseyside, Strathclyde and South Yorkshire have taken relatively small numbers.

Municipal fleets have been more enthusiastic although the sales potential is usually less. Lothian has been a big user of big Olympians, 128 with 10.2m (33ft 5in) ECW bodies delivered between 1982 and 1986. Other buyers have included Cardiff, Colchester, Derby, Grampian, Grimsby-Cleethorpes, Lincoln, Nottingham, Northampton, Preston, Reading, Southampton and Warrington.

SBG fleets were early Olympian users, and between 1980 and 1986 received more than 160, now spread between eight fleets.

After its Titan experience London was a potential Olympian customer and in 1984 took three experimental vehicles as part of an evaluation test involving the Dennis Dominator, MCW Metrobus II and Volvo Ailsa.

Although results from these tests were not available at the time, London ordered 260 Olympians with ECW two-door bodywork for 1986/87 delivery.

Few independents buy new double-deck buses now, but A1, Metrobus and South Yorkshire Road Transport have all bought Olympians.

Top:
The standard NBC Olympian is typified by this West Riding 1985 ONLXB/1R with 77-seat ECW body, in this case in West Yorkshire MetroBus livery. R. L. Wilson

Right:
Southampton bought two of these coach-seated long-wheelbase Olympians in 1986, with East Lancs 76-seat bodywork.
Roy Marshall

13 Dennis Falcon V

Wheelbase: 5.64m (18ft 6in)
Engine: Mercedes-Benz OM421 V6 10.96-litre six-cylinder
Rating: 188bhp @ 2,000rpm
Gearbox: Voith D851, 3-speed fully-automatic
Retarder: Integral
Brakes: Full air-operated service brakes
Steering gear: Integrally-powered
Rear axle: GKN straight-beam hub reduction
Suspension: Semi-elliptic leaf springs
Options: Full air suspension

The Model

In the 1980s, Hestair Dennis was enthusiastically tackling the bus market and had achieved some success with the Dominator and the Jubilant export chassis. In the 1980s the Falcon range was introduced with two basic models: the Falcon H and Falcon V.

The Falcon H was primarily intended as a single-deck model in the Bristol RELL mould and has sold in respectable numbers to municipal fleets; it featured a horizontal Gardner 6HLXB (or turbocharged 6HLXCT) engine.

The Falcon V could be used for either single-deck or double-deck bodywork and in double-deck form featured the Mercedes-Benz OM422 V8 engine. This compact unit allowed the engine to be placed under the floor at the rear.

The Market

Only five Falcon Vs have been delivered to British operators: two in 1983 to Nottingham and three in 1984 to Greater Manchester.

Above right:
Nottingham bought two of these Dennis Falcon V in 1982, fitted with East Lancs 88-seat bodywork to the undertaking's distinctive style. Malcolm Keeley

Right:
One of Greater Manchester PTE's three Dennis Falcon V at Atherton depot in 1984. The length of the vehicle, with 84-seat Northern Counties body, is apparent when compared with the Atlantean behind.
R. L. Wilson

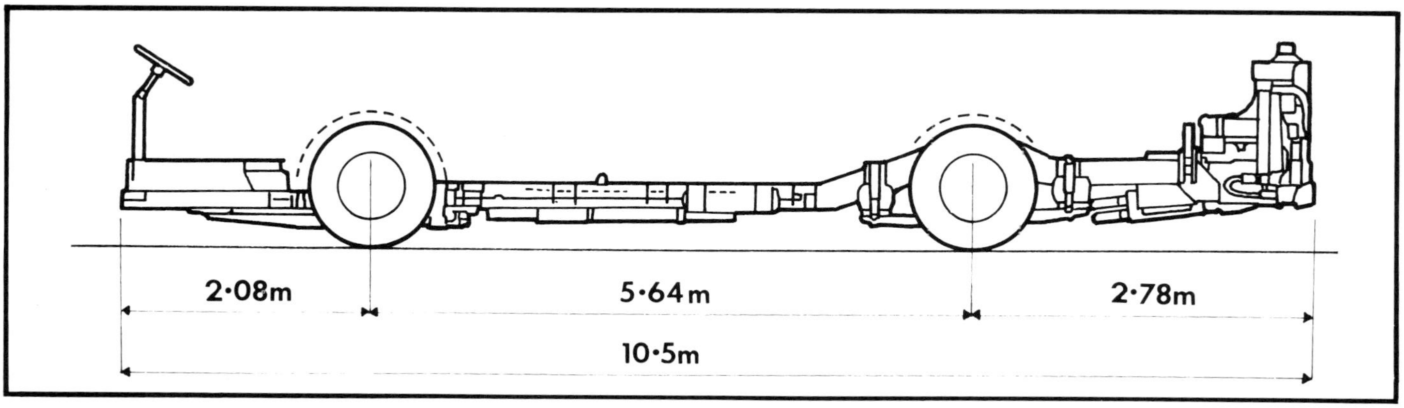

14 Double-Deck Coaches

The Models

Although this book is principally concerned with double-deck *buses* it is difficult to ignore the recent trend to double-deck coaches.

There has been a limited market for double-deck coaches since the 1920s and in more recent years the Ribble group companies have been the most enthusiastic users. These have been Leyland Titans and Atlanteans with suitably furnished and decorated versions of standard bodies, and the 30 Bristol VRLs bought in 1968-72.

While these have been mainly adaptations of standard models, a new breed of specially-designed double-deck coach has appeared from the continent in the 1980s.

The first was the Auwarter Neoplan Skyliner, a 12m (39ft 4in) three-axle West German design with rear-mounted Mercedes-Benz OM403 V10 engine, an exotic looking coach produced to the standard continental height of 4m (13ft 1in). This model has been particularly successful in Britain and since 1981 over 80 have entered service with such operators as Stagecoach, Trathens and Yelloway. In 1984 the Gardner 6LYT engine became an option and the DAF DKT is also offered.

The next import was the Belgian Van Hool Astromega, whose most notable customer has been Southend Transport. It too featured a Mercedes engine, in this case the V8 OM422 unit.

Inevitably, British manufacturers decided to fight back and Leyland produced a long wheelbase two-axle Olympian with ECW bodywork for NBC. This has been produced in both normal-height and low-height form.

While the Olympian was rather obviously based on an existing model, MCW's three-axle Metroliner of 1982 had virtually started with a clean sheet and was a model close to the continental designs. It was initially chosen by SBG and NBC companies for long-distance express work and later also joined the Tyne & Wear, West Midlands and London Coaches fleets.

Plaxtons built its first double-decker in 1984, a 4m (13ft 1in) high vehicle, the Paramount 4000, on a Neoplan under-

Right:
The Neoplan Skyliner was the first of the new-type double-deck coach designs to appear in service with British operators. This Yelloway example shows the distinctive styling of the Neoplan, and the three-axle layout. Roger Kaye

Below:
Possibly the most unusual municipal double-deckers of recent years have been the Van Hool Astromegas of Southend Transport. They are used on the X1 express service between Southend and Heathrow. The 12m length is very obvious in this 1983 view.
S. J. Butler

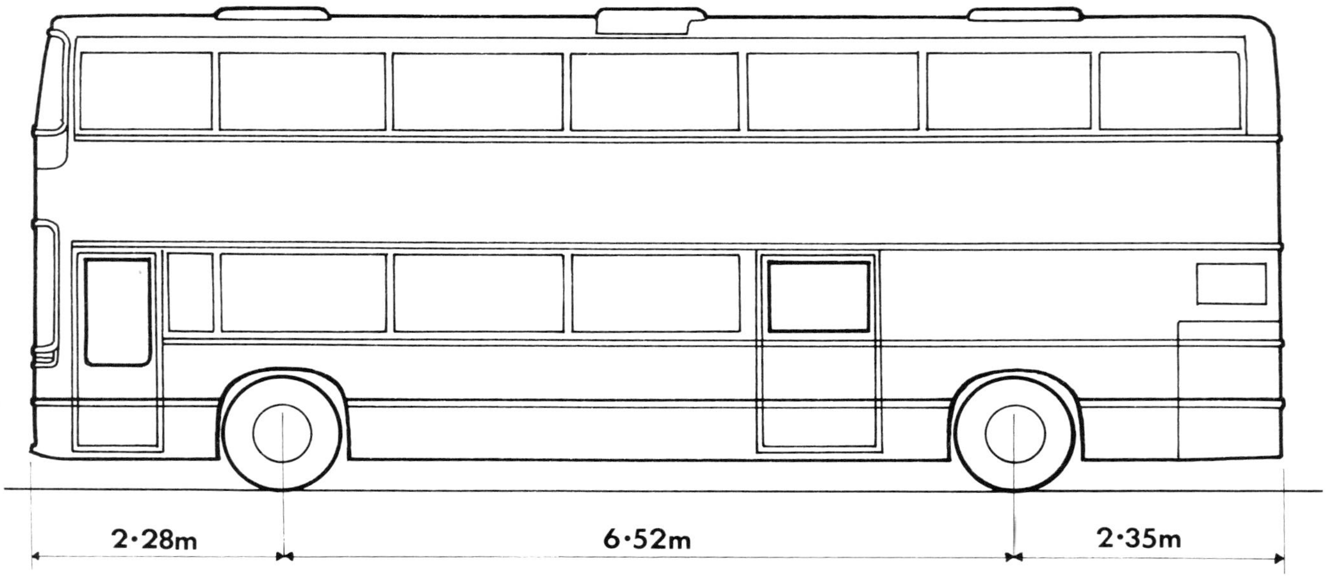

Leyland Olympian

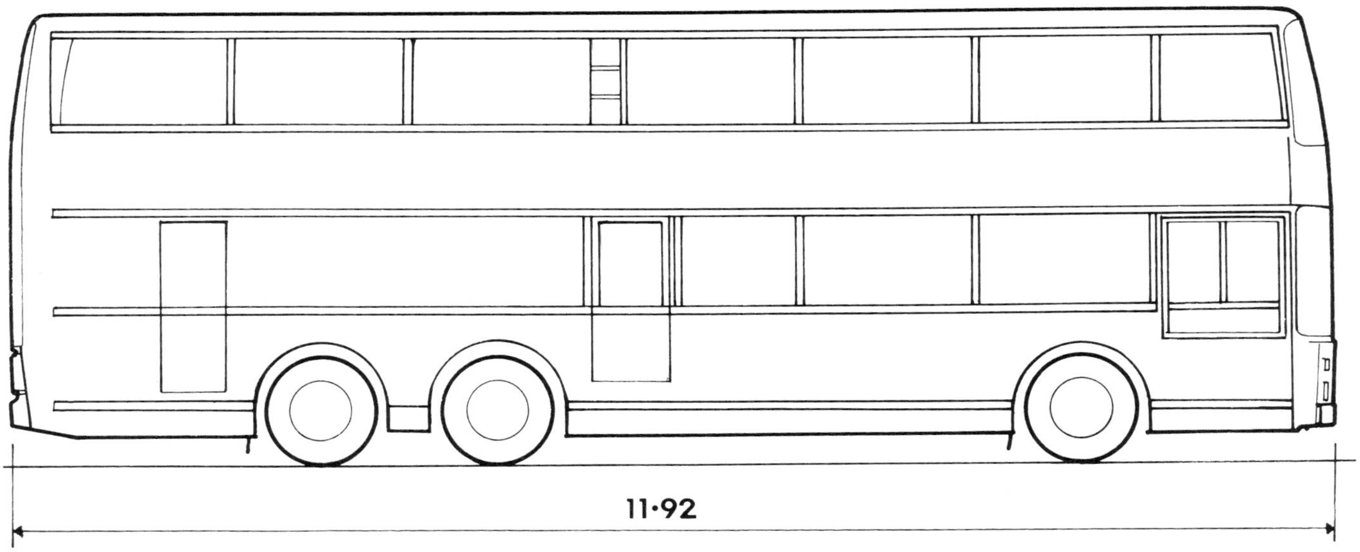

MCW Metroliner

frame. Other Plaxton 4000s have been built using Volvo B10M (underfloor-engined) or Scania K112 chassis.

In 1983 Setra introduced its Imperial double-deck model in Britain, an impressive but expensive vehicle.

The most recent double-deck coach model has been MCW's 400GT Metroliner, a 4m (13ft 1in) high vehicle, with a choice of in-line Gardner 6LYT or Cummins NTE engines.

In a slightly different category are the coach-specification double-deckers built using standard body shells suitably trimmed and fitted out. Most British coachbuilders have built these, from vehicles that were little more than buses with high-backed seats, through to plushly-furnished coaches for long-distance work.

The Market

The imported double-deck coaches have tended to attract the independent operators, whether for longer-distance express work or summer shuttle trips, while the Olympian and Metroliner sales have been in the public sector.

Municipal, PTE, SBG and independent operators have all taken coach-seated double-deckers in the 1980s.

Left:
Leyland Olympians with extra-long wheelbase (6.53m) were built for NBC companies with coach bodies by ECW. This Alder Valley 1983 example, one of five, was an ONTL11/2R model. S. J. Butler

Above right:
Eastern National received similar long-wheelbase Olympians with ECW coach bodies in 1985, but built to low-height size. They were ONTL11/2RSp, with space for 73 passengers. S. J. Butler

Right:
SBG took two of the longer-wheelbase Olympians and fitted Alexander RDC bodies for Eastern Scottish in 1984. John Burnett

Left:
The first MCW Metroliner coach was built for SBG, and was followed by similar vehicles for other Group fleets. Malcolm Keeley

Below:
The luggage compartment above the rear axles is shown in this view of an Ambassador Travel Metroliner 72-seat coach, new in 1986. Roy Marshall

Bottom:
London Buses bought four MCW Metroliners in 1986 for the express service between London and Birmingham operated jointly with Central Coachways, the coaching arm of West Midlands Travel, who use similar vehicles. Roy Marshall

Right:
London also bought two Leyland Olympians in 1986 with East Lancs 70-seat coach bodies, for the express service to Eastbourne. S. J. Butler

Below right:
The London Olympians were almost identical to the two vehicles bought a year earlier by joint operator Eastbourne. S. J. Butler

London Liner
PRIVATE CHARTER
London Liner
Leyland
C202 DYE

London Liner
London Liner
PRIVATE HIRE
2
B102 PHC

Left:
This Olympian coach with ECW body was shown at the 1984 Motor Show in Ebdon's colours, but was sold in 1985 to South Yorkshire PTE, and painted in Super Coachline livery. M. Fowler

Below:
Many regard the Setra Imperial as the Rolls-Royce of double-deck coaches, an expensive model that has been placed in service with several coach fleets. This Imperial was for Carnell of Sheffield, a company that went into liquidation in 1986. Roger Kaye

Bottom:
In addition to Metroliners, NBC fleets have taken delivery of Plaxton Paramount 4000 coaches, based on Neoplan underframes. This 1986 Yorkshire Traction example was one of five with Gardner 6LYT engines. The family resemblance to other Plaxton Paramount coaches is evident. S. J. Butler

Off-the-Peg Problems

The London Transport 2,646-strong DMS class caused problems for many people. This 'off-the-peg' model based on the Daimler Fleetline did not perform well in London, and seemed unsuited to LT's maintenance system. The size of London's order delayed Fleetline deliveries to other operators. And when LT decided to sell the vehicles prematurely, they were quickly snapped up by a wide variety of operators, who chose these in some cases instead of new buses, further depressing the new bus market. The ghost of the DMS has haunted the British bus scene since 1970, and this photo feature shows some of the many new homes for these buses.

Top:
The first of the class, DMS1, a Fleetline CRG6LX with Park Royal two-door body, seen when new. Park Royal

Right:
A sight that became familiar in the 1970s in London, a broken-down Fleetline — this one a CRL6 with MCW bodywork. Stewart J. Brown

Left:
The Ensign yard at Purfleet in 1984, with London Fleetlines in various states of repair.
Ian Cowley

Below left:
Chesterfield bought 16 CRL6 Fleetlines from London with Park Royal bodywork.
Malcolm Keeley

Below:
Another municipal customer — Grimsby Cleethorpes, and one of 20 CRG6LX with MCW bodywork bought in 1982/83.
Roy Marshall

Left:
Independent Lockey of Evenwood bought this 1972 CRG6LXB with MCW body in 1980 from nearby operator OK of Bishop Auckland.
Roy Marshall

Above right:
Graham's of Paisley had before the DMS mostly bought new double-deckers, but the London model appeared to suit its needs and became the standard purchase.
Stewart J. Brown

Right:
West Midlands PTE bought 80 DMSs, typified by two CRG6LXB with MCW 71-seat bodies.
Roger Kaye

Below:
Stevenson of Uttoxeter has also built up a substantial fleet of DMSs, like this 1972 CRG6LXB/Park Royal seen in Burton in 1984.
R. L. Wilson

Right:
The Leicester-based Midland Fox company also found the DMS a useful buy, including third-hand examples from other NBC fleets. This is a Fleetline CRL6 with MCW body.
Roy Marshall

Below:
The DMS class was also useful for Western National, with a peak summertime need for double-deckers in Cornwall; this example is seen in St Ives in 1986. M. Fowler

Below right:
Premier of Cambridge bought DMSs in 1985, its first double-deckers for some years. This is a Fleetline FE30LR with Park Royal body.
Ian Cowley

Bottom:
Not a DMS, but built at the same time, one of 29 Fleetline FE30AGR for South Yorkshire PTE in 1977 with MCW 71-seat two-door bodywork. Mike Greenwood

Alternatives to the Rear-Engined Double-Decker

The only real alternative to the double-deck bus in the early 1970s was the high-capacity single-decker, but while some operators were happy with this solution most stuck to double-deckers. Leyland was for a while the only company building double-deck chassis and dissatisfaction with this situation brought two new models into competition. One was the MCW Metropolitan, described earlier, and the other was the Ailsa, a new *front*-engined underframe.

The Ailsa had little in common with the previous generation of front-engined double-deckers. It had a perimeter-frame chassis for mounting an integrated body structure, but the main novelty was the Volvo TD70 engine, a compact unit mounted to the left of the driving position with enough space for a front platform. Guy had used a similar layout with its Wulfrunian model in 1959, but this incorporated other advanced features as well as the rather bulky Gardner 6LX engine and these did not help its chances. The Ailsa was an altogether simpler model, and enjoyed a modest success, taking 7% of the double-deck market in its best year, 1976, and remaining in production from 1974 until 1984.

There was a brief interest in articulated single-deck buses as an alternative to double-deckers, and in the early 1980s South Yorkshire PTE, British Airways and Luton Airport took artics, but these totalled only 20 buses. South Yorkshire bought a further 13 in 1985.

Volvo resisted the temptation to produce a rear-engined double-decker for the British market. Its single-deck city buses, familiar in many parts of Europe, were rear-engined, the B59 and B10R, but the company firmly believed in mid-mounted horizontal engines for its coach range, and using the highly-successful B10M chassis as a base developed the Citybus underfloor-engined double-deck model.

Others had tried to produce a practical underfloor double-deck chassis before: AEC had experimented with the Regent IV in 1949-50, and Midland Red with the D10 in 1959-61, but without real success.

The Volvo Citybus had an unusually low frame, which helped it to succeed where others had not. It was introduced at a difficult time for double-deck sales, in 1982 when the peak deliveries had passed, but has made its presence felt — not least at Leyland who were moved to produce an equivalent model. This used a chassis built by DAB, Leyland's Danish subsidiary, and was marketed as the Leyland Lion; it too came at a bad time, when the whole market was depressed.

Below:
The first Midland Red D10 underfloor-engined double-decker on its first day in service in January 1961, leaving Coventry's Pool Meadow bus station. The second bus had two doors, with the second behind the rear axle.
T. W. Moore

Above:
South Yorkshire PTE bought 62 of the front-engined Volvo Ailsa in 1976, with Irish-built Van Hool McArdle bodywork, and at the same time were buying rear-engined models like the 1973 Fleetline/Park Royal on the right (actually an ex-Sheffield bus). M. Fowler

This picture:
The third of London Transport's experimental Volvo Ailsas in 1984 had an Alexander R-type body with a second staircase and a second door, possible because of the mechanical layout of the model. Alexander

Double-Deck Bodywork

The number of builders providing bodywork on double-deck buses has fallen as the market has reduced.

In 1970 there were eight British firms chasing the business: Alexander, ECW, East Lancs, MCW, Northern Counties, Park Royal, Roe and Willowbrook. By 1984 Park Royal, Roe and Willowbrook had fallen by the wayside and ECW built its last bodies in 1987. Two new names appeared in the meantime: Marshall, normally associated with single-deck bodywork, started offering double-deck bodies from 1978, and Van Hool McArdle, a Dublin-based offshoot of the Belgian Van Hool empire, was set up to build bodies for Coras Iompair Eireann, and in 1976/77 built bodies for British operators before it went bankrupt. Since that time Optare has risen from the ashes of the Roe business at Leeds.

Bus operators have tended to have their own favourite body suppliers, though cost has become an increasingly important consideration, resulting in some interesting switches of allegiance.

The most prolific single builder of double-deck bodies in the years since 1970 has been MCW. At the start of the period MCW was heavily involved with single-deck bodies, but since 1975 the number of double-deck bodies jumped considerably, helped by substantial London and West Midlands orders on Daimler Fleetline chassis and then by the success of the integral Metrobus.

MCW has tended to chase big orders and has been more likely to supply bigger operators like London, the PTEs and the large municipalities. Orders from NBC companies were rare until the Metrobus started to attract business. MCW's double-deck output averaged over 350 buses a year since 1970.

The second busiest double-deck bodybuilder has been Eastern Coach Works, which built more than 5,000 bodies in the period from 1970, an average of more than 300 a year and an actual output of over 600 in the record year, 1980.

NBC fleets took the bulk of ECW's production, but there have also been occasional PTE and SBG orders and London's Olympians. Municipalities, many in the south and east, have been faithful ECW customers and a surprise

Right:
Metro-Cammell built bodies largely for bigger customers, like Merseyside PTE — a 1973 Fleetline CRG6LXB, one of 50.
Malcolm Keeley

Below:
Although most Eastern Coach Works business was for NBC fleets, some bodies were built for independents. This 1980 Bristol VRT/SL6G with ECW 70 coach seat body for Stevenson of Uttoxeter, was followed by another in 1981. Alongside was one of the prototype Leyland Olympians, also with ECW body, and Bristol VRT-style front grille. R. L. Wilson

Right:
Alexander traditionally supplied SBG and Scottish municipal customers, and expanded to build for a much wider range of fleets. A Lothian Region 1977 Leyland Atlantean AN68A/1R with 75-seat body.
Stewart J. Brown

Below right:
Park Royal's closure was accelerated by problems with the integral Leyland Titan model. This was one of 15 Park Royal-built Titans delivered to Greater Manchester PTE in 1978. Roger Kaye

convert was Lothian with orders for over 120 10.2m (33ft 5in) Olympians.

Walter Alexander's double-deck body output has varied with the whims of its main customers, usually SBG and the PTEs, but it has averaged over 300 a year for the home market since 1970.

Merseyside, South Yorkshire, Strathclyde and Tyne & Wear have all been good Alexander customers, but municipalities have been more fickle with one-time Alexander regulars like Bournemouth, Lothian, Portsmouth and Tayside turning to English suppliers.

Park Royal was once one of the most respected and most prolific of British bodybuilders; as recently as 1972/73 it was normally turning out more than 500 double-deck bodies annually for the home market. Like MCW, Park Royal had specialised in long-run orders for major customers; SELNEC/Greater Manchester and West Midlands were big Park Royal fans in the 1970s, but London Transport was, as ever, the main customer, with large batches of DM class Fleetlines. Park Royal gained some useful NBC business on Leyland Atlantean to help counteract a shortage of Bristol VRTs. Latterly, Park Royal was assembling the integral Leyland Titan, but labour problems meant that Leyland decided to close the Park Royal factory and transfer Titan production to Workington.

Northern Counties production rose steadily in the years since 1970, to peak in 1978-81 when more than 200 double-deckers were bodied in each year. The company's close links with SELNEC/ Greater Manchester meant that over three-quarters of production was for the PTE. Other PTEs and municipals took deliveries when they could. The last NBC deliveries were in 1972 and SBG took 50 bodies in 1978/79.

Leyland closed the Roe coachworks in 1984 and output during the previous 15 years had averaged over 120 double-deck bodies a year. Roe was very much linked with the Leeds municipal fleet and its successor West Yorkshire PTE; in a typical year around half the production was for West Yorkshire, with other Yorkshire undertakings accounting for much of the rest. Some NBC business on Atlantean was diverted from Park Royal, and normal-height Olympians were built for Bristol Omnibus and London Country. Independents often went to Roe for double-deck bodies where other builders were less interested in one-off orders.

A new coachbuilder, Optare, was created in the Crossgates factory and while it has built some double-deckers for West Yorkshire PTE, it has been most successful with smaller buses.

East Lancashire Coach Builders also had a largely local following and a steady output averaging just over 100 bodies a year. Some PTE business was won, but East Lancs has tended to be most closely associated with municipal fleets. While many have been in the northwest of England, the company has successfully won business in areas far from home — in Tayside, and along the south coast of England (Bournemouth, Brighton, Eastbourne, Plymouth, Portsmouth, Southampton).

Other double-deck bodybuilders in the period made little real impact on the market. Willowbrook had been around as a double-deck builder for some years, but between 1970 and 1982 sold varying quantities to PTEs, municipal and even NBC fleets. Van Hool McArdle had been formed to build bodies in Dublin for CIE, and in 1976/77 it picked up an order for South Yorkshire PTE, diverted from Alexander because of production delays. Marshall came late into the double-deck field, in 1978, and has mainly sold to municipal and PTE customers; its double-deck sales have been modest, reaching a peak of 41 in 1981.

The only other significant force in the British double-deck bus body market has been Leyland, whose Titan model was transferred from Park Royal to the

Workington assembly plant in Cumbria. Production started there in 1981, and by 1984 over 880 had been built. The model was discontinued when London Transport switched its orders to the MCW Metrobus.

With a home double-deck market well below half of its 1980/81 peak, it was inevitable that there would be casualties among the bodybuilders, though the demise of Leyland's ECW, Park Royal and Roe factories has greatly reduced choice.

The remaining builders have tried to diversify to counteract the drop in double-deck demand. Alexander has its successful export business, and has built batches of railcars for British Rail. East Lancs has become more involved with single-deck and small buses than in the past, and has built tramcars for Blackpool. MCW has gone into coaches, and in 1986 developed the 25-seat Metrorider midibus. Northern Counties has also become involved in smaller buses.

Top:
Much of the output from Northern Counties has been for Greater Manchester, but at one time it also won BET group and NBC orders. This low-height Fleetline was new to City of Oxford in 1968. Daimler

Above left:
A South Yorkshire PTE Leyland Atlantean AN68A/1R of 1979, restored to Sheffield Transport livery, photographed outside the Roe coachworks at Leeds, where its body was built, after the closure of the works.
Roger Kaye

Left:
East Lancs bodywork is favoured by a wide range of municipal and independent customers. This 75-seat body on Dennis Dominator DDA100S chassis was one of four for Brighton in 1986. Roy Marshall

Evaluation

Most evaluation of new double-deck bus types is carried out in service. Some bus operators might try a demonstrator, but others buy on promise or reputation. Occasionally an operator will conduct proper evaluation tests, comparing its normal model with other models on the market. These can give a useful chance to see how different types perform in similar situations, though it should be remembered that many factors affect the acceptance of a bus in a particular fleet, not least the attitudes and prejudices of local traffic and maintenance staff.

One of the first full-scale tests involving rear-engined double-deckers was carried out in 1965. Edinburgh Corporation was one of the biggest municipalities that had resisted the temptation of Atlanteans and Fleetlines, and stuck to the front-engined Leyland Titan with over 420 in the fleet.

Four buses were used in the comparisons — Leyland Atlantean, Daimler Fleetline, AEC Renown and one of Edinburgh's own Titan PD3s. The Renown was AEC's latest double-deck model, a low-height front-engined chassis, successor to the integral Bridgemaster.

The buses were used on three routes for four days each, and as well as fuel consumption records, crew and passenger reaction was sought. The Renown returned the best fuel consumption, but was felt to offer little more, and next came the Leyland PD3. The rear-engined buses were next, with little difference between them. The outcome was a recommendation that the next order should be split between Atlanteans and Fleetlines, but Edinburgh decided to play safe and order 25 Atlanteans and 25 Titan PD3s; these were to be Edinburgh's last Titans, though, and the Atlantean became the standard purchase. (See Table 1.)

Table 1

Edinburgh Corporation Tests, 1965 — Fuel Consumption

AEC Renown	8.56mpg	Daimler Fleetline	8.25mpg
Leyland Atlantean	8.2mpg	Leyland Titan PD3	8.46mpg

Later in 1965 Halifax Corporation carried out a series of comparative evaluation tests to find a double-decker suitable for that hilly and difficult area. Buses from the Halifax fleet, an AEC Regent V, Daimler CVG6 and Leyland Titan PD3, were compared with a selection of current double-deck types. There were front-engined buses: an AEC Renown, Dennis Loline, Guy Arab V and a forward-entrance Routemaster. And there were two Atlanteans and a Fleetline representing the rear-engined lobby. The buses were to spend seven days in turn on one of three Halifax routes, chosen for the varying characteristics.

The best fuel consumption was returned by the Halifax Daimler CVG6, fitted with a Gardner 6LX engine, followed by one of the Atlanteans, a demonstrator, although the other Atlantean, from Wallasey, was second poorest.

Following these tests Halifax ordered Dennis Lolines, a model that had performed well, and then followed these with more Leyland PD2s and some Daimler Fleetlines. (See Table 2.)

Table 2

Halifax Corporation Tests, 1965 — Fuel Consumption

AEC Regent V	8.77mpg	AEC Renown	9.15mpg
AEC Routemaster	9.25mpg	Daimler CVG6LX	9.80mpg
Daimler Fleetline	9.27mpg	Dennis Loline	8.59mpg
Guy Arab V	8.32mpg	Leyland Atlantean (demonstrator)	9.45mpg
Leyland Atlantean (Wallasey)	8.36mpg	Leyland Titan PD3	8.82mpg

NBC, with a sizeable annual intake of double-deckers, found itself in the mid-1970s with a wider market choice than previously. Its standard model was the Bristol VRT, its constituent companies had long experience of Atlanteans and Fleetlines, but there was a new generation of models on the market.

So in 1976 a batch of buses was allocated to Maidstone & District for direct comparisons during a two-year trial. These were five Ailsas, five MCW Metropolitans, and four Bristol VRT/SL3s (two with Gardner 6LXB engines and two with Leyland 510 engines). The buses were first used in Hastings and then transferred to Chatham, and throughout passenger and staff opinions were sought, in addition to the normal monitoring of performance.

Passengers rated the air suspension Metropolitan best, followed by the VRTs and the Ailsas. In terms of performance the Gardner-engined Bristols came out on top, followed by the Ailsas, the Leyland-engined VRTs and the Metropolitans. The fuel consumption figures are shown in the table below.

The 1978 report on the tests stated: 'In this age of rising costs and fall in passengers, the two factors of prime concern must be low operating costs and vehicle reliability. The Gardner-engined Bristol VRT has shown up well in both respects.'

On the basis of operating costs, the Gardner VRTs were the cheapest to run (at £90.82 per 1,000 miles) followed by the Ailsas (£108.71), the Leyland VRTs (£109.24) and the Metropolitans (£113.30).

NBC was no doubt relieved that the tests confirmed that its standard model was a good choice; in the event, NBC bought no more Ailsas or Metropolitans. (See Table 3.)

In July 1978 South Yorkshire PTE commenced an ambitious three-month test programme in Sheffield with five vehicles. Three were SYPTE buses, a Dennis Dominator, Foden-NC and Volvo Ailsa Mk 2; the others were demonstrators, a Leyland Titan and MCW Metrobus.

The Dominator and Metrobus each had Rolls-Royce engines and the Dominator, Metrobus and Ailsa all had Voith transmission. The five buses were used on South Yorkshire's testing eight-mile long route 51 from Herdings, climbing to Lodge Moor, 1,000ft above sea level, and the first results showed that the Titan returned the best fuel consumption — though it did not compare so well in other areas. Poorest on

Table 3

NBC Tests, 1976-78 — Fuel Consumption

Bristol VRT (Gardner)	7.94mpg	Bristol VRT (Leyland)	6.92mpg
MCW Metropolitan	6.72mpg	Volvo Ailsa	6.72mpg

Above and below:
During the Edinburgh evaluation tests, Daimler Fleetline demonstrator 565 CRW with Alexander bodywork, and KTD 551C the Leyland Atlantean/Park Royal demonstrator.
Stewart J. Brown

fuel consumption was the Ailsa, although this bus was rated high on accessibility and came second in driver's preference and reliability.

First driver's choice was the Dominator, which rated third on reliability. The Metrobus had the poorest reliability and was fourth on driver appeal. Titan was fourth for reliability and bottom on driver preference.

The Foden turned out to be most reliable, though drivers placed it third and engineers were reported to be 'surprised at the efficiency' of the Ferodo retarder.

South Yorkshire's subsequent orders were mainly for Dominators, though Metrobuses and Atlanteans were also bought, all with Voith gearboxes. (See Table 4.)

SBG carried out two-stage vehicle evaluations in the Glasgow area in 1980/81. The first stage in 1980 involved the Daimler Fleetline, SBG's standard double-deck model, and three of the newer types, the Ailsa, Dominator and Metrobus. All were vehicles from SBG fleets, though the Dominator and Metrobus were experimental vehicles. The six-month trial revealed that the Fleetline returned the best fuel consumption, and the best overall availability for service at 95.6%. In terms of fuel consumption, the Metrobus came next, followed by the Dominator and Ailsa. The Dominator had the poorest availability — it only performed 70% of its scheduled mileage. SBG's subsequent vehicle orders included all of the three newer models.

The second stage, a year later, involved the Ailsa, Fleetline and Metrobus, in comparison with the Leyland Olympian, then newly introduced. The same route was used, between central Glasgow and suburban Drumchapel, and the tests showed that the Olympian emerged with the best fuel consumption of the new generation type — but the Fleetline still returned the best consumption. Availability of the Olympian at over 97% was slightly better than the Fleetline (95.7%), followed by the Ailsa (80.7%) and Metrobus (70.5%).

SBG's vehicle-buying policy allowed individual companies to choose the models they favoured, so Ailsa, Metrobus and Olympian all featured in future orders. (See Table 5.)

Strathclyde PTE had inherited a large fleet of Leyland Atlanteans, and had bought experimental batches of some of the newer types. Batches of three types were used in trials in 1981/82 from the Maryhill garage — 10 Ailsas, two Metrobuses and 10 Olympians. At the end of the third phase in the tests, the Metrobus had returned the best fuel consumption, followed closely by the Ailsa fitted with the Voith gearbox, the Ailsa with SCG box and the Olympian. In service, the Ailsa proved most reliable (83.42% availability), followed by the Olympian and Metrobus. Although the Metrobus was most economical in fuel terms, repair and maintenance costs were 60% higher than the Olympian.

Strathclyde continued to triple-source its orders but favoured the Ailsa for its bulk orders. (See Table 6.)

Table 4

South Yorkshire PTE Tests, 1978 — Fuel Consumption

Dennis Dominator	5.4mpg	Foden-NC	5.8mpg
Leyland Titan	6.5mpg	MCW Metrobus	5.8mpg
Volvo Ailsa	5.1mpg		

Table 5

SBG Tests, 1980/81 — Fuel Consumption

First Test (1980)		*Second Test (1981)*	
Daimler Fleetline	7.26mpg	Daimler Fleetline	7.36mpg
Dennis Dominator	6.03mpg	Leyland Olympian	6.51mpg
MCW Metrobus	6.2mpg	MCW Metrobus	6.14mpg
Volvo Ailsa	5.8mpg	Volvo Ailsa	5.82mpg

Table 6

Strathclyde PTE Tests, 1981/82 — Fuel Consumption

Leyland Olympian	5.88mpg	MCW Metrobus	6.31mpg
Volvo Ailsa (SCG)	6.02mpg	Volvo Ailsa (Voith)	6.29mpg

Below:
Two of the buses featured in the South Yorkshire tests — the prototype Dennis Dominator/East Lancs and the Foden/East Lancs. M. Fowler

Keeping their Options Open

With such a wide choice of double-deck models from the 1970s, some operators protected their interests and bought from more than one manufacturer. Dual-sourcing helped some fleets to get through the difficult days of chassis shortage and body delays in the 1970s, and for the biggest fleets, with a sizeable annual vehicle requirement, it safeguarded deliveries.

But while dual-sourcing was a fairly widespread practice, and some fleets stayed loyal to just one model, others tried a little of everything, mainly to get experience of the choices, to help formulate future vehicle policy.

The most significant multi-sourcing was carried out by Greater Manchester PTE and its predecessor SELNEC. With the Atlantean as the basic model it has bought significant numbers of Fleetlines and Dominators and GM Buses now appears to have standardised on the Olympian and Metrobus — but along the way it has tried at least nominal batches of every other double-deck model, except (so far) the Leyland Lion.

The other PTEs have been almost as diverse in their choices. Merseyside, again principally an Atlantean fleet, has tried most of the newer types in small numbers, but has not placed a significant double-deck order for some time.

Tyne & Wear, previously a big Atlantean customer, now chooses Olympian.

Right:
Representing the variety of types in the Greater Manchester PTE fleet — all with Northern Counties bodies: a Volvo Ailsa of 1982, one of three; a 1978 Lancashire United Fleetline FE30AGR; and a 1982 Leyland-engined Olympian. The LUT fleet passed to GM in 1981, although new vehicles had latterly been to Manchester design.
Roger Kaye

Below:
Three West Midlands PTE types at Oldbury in 1984: a 1976 Volvo Ailsa/Alexander; a 1982 MCW Metrobus Mk II; and a 1975 Fleetline/ Park Royal. S. J. Butler

West Midlands has been particularly single-minded with huge fleets of Fleetlines and then Metrobuses, but has also tried VRTs, Ailsas and Titans and a solitary Foden.

Strathclyde inherited Glasgow's big Atlantean fleet, but dissatisfaction led to purchases of Ailsas and Metropolitans and more recently Metrobuses and Olympians.

West Yorkshire was another PTE Atlantean customer who turned to Olympians and Metrobuses, but not before it had tried Metropolitans, a Foden and an Ailsa along the way. South Yorkshire PTE has tended to plough its own furrow, becoming the biggest Dominator customer via several other types.

The big PTEs had the best chance to buy buses of different types, but some of the municipal fleets have been equally prodigious. Inevitably it has been the bigger municipalities, like Cardiff, Derby, Leicester, Nottingham and Tayside, that have been able to switch orders between manufacturers.

NBC's centrally-controlled vehicle-buying policy has tended to restrict the variety of types in any single fleet, and only Maidstone & District and Northern General have a greater choice of types; the Maidstone fleet, of course, was used for NBC's vehicle evaluation tests.

SBG has allowed its companies a freer hand and two fleets, Central and Eastern, have bought examples of several different double-deck models.

London has had a surprising number of types through its hands. It is easy to think of London as a highly-standardised fleet, and forget the experimental Atlanteans, the rear-engined Routemaster, and the more recent test buses.

The table below shows the fleets that have bought new examples of most double-deck models.

	Atlantean	*Fleetline*	*VRT*	*Metropolitan*	*Foden*	*Titan*	*Dominator*	*Metrobus*	*Scania*	*Olympian*	*Falcon V*	*Ailsa*	*Citybus*	*Lion*
Greater Manchester	●	●	●	●	●	●	●	●	●	●	●	●	●	
London Transport	●	●		●		●	●	●		●		●	●	
South Yorkshire	●	●	●	●	●		●	●		●		●		
Maidstone & District	●	●	●	●			●	●		●		●		
Merseyside	●	●	●	●			●	●		●		●		
Derby		●			●		●	●		●		●	●	
Nottingham	●	●							●	●	●		●	●
Strathclyde	●	●		●				●		●		●	●	
Tyne & Wear	●	●		●				●	●	●		●		
West Midlands	●	●	●		●	●		●				●		
West Yorkshire	●	●		●	●			●		●		●		
Cardiff	●	●	●				●			●		●		
Eastern Scottish		●	●							●		●	●	●
Tayside		●	●				●	●				●	●	
Central Scottish		●	●				●			●		●		
Leicester	●			●			●	●	●					
Northern General	●	●	●					●		●				

Bottom:
Three London bus types at Aldgate in 1985: a standard Routemaster; a 1979 Titan/Park Royal; and a 1981 MCW Metrobus. Ian Cowley